ALSO BY ICE-T

The Ice Opinion

ICE

A MEMOIR OF GANGSTER LIFE AND

REDEMPTION—FROM SOUTH CENTRAL TO HOLLYWOOD

ICE-T
and
DOUGLAS CENTURY

ONE WORLD • BALLANTINE BOOKS • NEW YORK

Published in the United States by One World Books,
an imprint of The Random House Publishing Group,
a division of Random House, Inc., New York.

ONE WORLD is a registered trademark and
the One World colophon is a trademark of Random House, Inc.

Permission credits for photographs and song lyrics can be found
beginning on page 253.

Library of Congress Cataloging-in-Publication Data
Ice-T (Musician)
Ice : a memoir of gangster life and redemption—from South Central
to Hollywood / Ice-T and Douglas Century.
       p.   cm.
ISBN 978-0-345-52328-0 (hardcover : alk. paper)—
ISBN 978-0-345-52330-3 (ebook)
1. Ice-T (Musician) 2. Rap musicians—United States—Biography.
I. Century, Douglas. II. Title.
ML420.I3A3 2011
782.421649092—dc22
      [B]   2010041069

Printed in the United States of America

www.oneworldbooks.net

2   4   6   8   9   7   5   3   1

First Edition

Book design by Christopher M. Zucker

ACKNOWLEDGMENTS

Special thanks to everyone who's supported me for twenty-five years and counting. My intent has always been to share and exchange game with players worldwide.

Love to all my fallen homeys, dead and locked away in prison. You are missed dearly.

Eternal love to my inner circle of friends, family, and my wife, who really know what I go through, and work to keep me focused and healthy.

Peace to all the young street hustlers, players, and gangstas. To win the game you must devise an exit strategy. We all saw the last scene in *Scarface.*

—Iceberg

AUTHOR'S NOTE

People have to learn how to tell stories without implicating those who may not want their stories told. Some names and situations have been changed to protect those involved.

PART ONE

COLD AS ICE

"IT'S HELL TO BE AN ORPHAN AT AN EARLY AGE
THIS IMPRESSIONABLE STAGE
NO LOVE BREEDS RAGE."

—"I MUST STAND"

1.

BECAUSE I FIRST MADE MY NAME as a rapper claiming South Central L.A., people often assume I'm strictly a West Coast cat. But my family was actually from back East. I was born in Newark, New Jersey, and grew up in Summit, an upscale town in north Jersey. There was this tiny area of Summit where most of the black families lived. My parents and I lived in a duplex house on Williams Street. And on the street right behind us—backyard to backyard—was my aunt, my father's sister.

For my first few years, it was just a real middle-American life.

I don't remember taking any trips or anything exciting. One thing I do remember, when my dad would take me places, he would get White Castle burgers and throw me in the backseat, and he expected me to eat my White Castles and be quiet. My dad and I spent a lot of time together not saying anything. I went to the YMCA, where I learned how to swim and do gymnastics. It was kind of a big deal to have a membership to the Y, because it meant your Pops had money to spend on you. I remember going from Pollywog to Dolphin, then graduating to

Shark and Lifesaver, and I'm pretty proud of the fact that I learned to be a good swimmer.

There wasn't any violence or trauma. It was quiet, simple, and suburban. An almost perfect childhood—except, for me, every couple years, losing a parent . . .

MY FATHER'S FAMILY CAME FROM Virginia and Philadelphia. He wasn't a brother who talked a lot. He was a workingman, a quiet, blue-collar dude. For years—decades—he worked at the same job. He was a skilled mechanic at the Rapistan Conveyer Company in Mountainside, fixing conveyer belts. Despite the fact that Summit is predominantly white, I can't say there was overt prejudice in the town, at least not within the adult world as I observed it. All my father's friends, all the guys he worked with, were white working-class dudes. Lunch-bucket dudes. Black and white, they were all cool with one another.

My father was a dark-skinned brother, but my mother was a very fair-skinned lady. From what I understand she was Creole; we think her people originally came from New Orleans. She looked almost like a white woman, which meant she could *pass*—as folks used to say back then. Her hair was jet-black. She was slim and very attractive. I recall people telling her she looked like Lena Horne or Dorothy Dandridge.

The fact that my mother could pass intrigued me, even as a little kid. I understood that it was a big fucking deal. In my household, it was often a topic of quiet discussion between my parents. When you can pass, you get to hear the way white people speak freely with one another when black folks aren't around. You get that kind of undercover look at the way white folks really think. So my mother understood racism intimately, from both sides of the fence, and there was never any tolerance for it in the house.

As hazy as a lot of my childhood is to me, I do have a very clear memory of the day when I first learned I was black. Before that, I guess, I never really *knew* I was black. Everybody figures out there's something called "race" at some point in their life, and for me it happened when I was about seven years old.

At the time, I was going to Brayton Elementary School in Summit, and I used to have a white friend named Alex. He was one of my closest friends in school. Alex and me were walking over to his house one day after school and we bumped into this other kid from our class named Kenneth—he was one of the few other black kids who went to Brayton with me. Soon as we ran into Kenneth, Alex told him, "Kenneth, you can't come over." Kenneth looked pretty bummed out but he just walked on, head down, kicking the curb the way little kids do. Then we ran into some more kids from our class and Alex had no problem inviting them to his house to play. We walked along the sidewalk in silence and the question just popped into my head.

"I thought you told Kenneth you couldn't have any more friends over?" I asked.

"Kenneth?" Alex laughed. "Oh, Kenneth—he's a darkie."

He said that shit so matter-of-fact. I didn't understand it. My mind was trippin' the rest of the afternoon.

Damn, I thought, *Alex must think I'm white. I guess I'm* passing, *too.*

Now, I had this other white friend named Mark, and the rules at his place were a little different than at Alex's. All the kids could come over to Mark's place to play in the yard, but when it got dark outside, as soon as the twilight made it hard to see, the white kids were allowed to come inside the house and keep playing but the black kids were sent home. Nobody asked any questions. Nobody said shit. It was just accepted as the way things were. And I was still considered "white enough"—or maybe they were just confused about what exactly I was—that I could stay and play with the white kids while the handful of black kids just split.

It was confusing as hell. When I got home, I told my mother about it. She looked at me with this half smile.

"Honey, people are stupid."

That was her line. It's one of the things I recall her saying to me a lot. *People are stupid.* She didn't break that down for me, but I understood her to mean: You can't necessarily change the ignorant way people think—but you can damn sure control the way it *affects* you personally. And then you keep it moving.

I guess my mom was preparing me in her own way, simply by down-playing it, telling me that this was some bullshit—racism—that I was going to be dealing with in some way or another for the rest of my life. Even today, I find myself constantly saying those same words under my breath: *Yo, don't even sweat it. People are stupid.*

MY MOTHER died of a sudden heart attack when I was in the third grade. I've read some craziness online that my parents were killed in a fiery car crash. No, they both died of heart attacks, four years apart. It was *me* that nearly died in a car wreck, but that was decades later, when I was already hustling out in Cali.

When my mother passed I didn't cry. To this day, I don't fully un-derstand why. I didn't shed any tears. I didn't go to the funeral, either. I didn't have much say in the matter. In those days, that's how grown folks handled kids when someone died. Someone—must have been my father—decided to keep me at the house, away from the church or the funeral home. All the younger kids—me and some cousins on my dad's side—were upstairs in our house playing the whole day. We were kind of oblivious. We never went downstairs with the mourners. I don't think it's quite the same today, but back then there was a conscious ef-fort to shelter kids more. You'd be sent upstairs, you might even be sent away to someone else's house, during the funeral arrangements.

The first time I ever cried in my life—the first time really letting out tears of grief—was at the funeral of my homey Vic. Victor Wilson—Beatmaster V, the drummer from my band Body Count. And that was in 1996, when I was a grown-ass man, after watching Vic's body get devastated by leukemia.

Even today, I don't dig the whole scene of a funeral. Funerals are ugly. I never go to them. I'd much rather remember the person alive. I don't want to see anybody lying in a box.

My mother didn't have any family around us. In fact, I never knew anybody from my mother's side of the family; even today I don't. My fa-ther, though, had two sisters and a lot of cousins. My aunt in the neigh-borhood had two daughters. There was a lot of family showing up at the house who I'd never seen before my mother's funeral.

All these folks—distant relations and friends—kept coming by to pay their respects. Also, I later found out: to steal stuff. That's the one thing I recall vividly after my mother's funeral. My father was pissed because a bunch of shit was missing from the house after it was all over.

MY MOTHER WAS a very supportive and smart woman, and I know she cared about me, although she wasn't very affectionate toward me. I only have a few specific memories of her, vague and distant, like some grainy home movie, someplace in the back of my mind. . . .

I'm sitting on the couch watching *Batman* on TV; she's calling out, "Tracy!" telling me to come to dinner . . .

I remember her sitting on the sofa a lot, with balls of yarn and knitting needles. That was my mother's only hobby; she loved to knit and crochet. I'd watch her making these intricate squares and then connecting them together into quilts. We had her quilts, neatly folded, on the beds and sofas in the house.

This may sound strange, but I don't know that much about my mother's personal story. I'm not a very backward-looking person. I realize that a lot of people like to dig into their past, research it, log in to genealogical websites to find out about their roots. I have no interest *whatsoever* in that shit. I've never been a guy to spend too long looking in the rearview mirror. To me it's like John Lennon once said: "I never went to high school reunions. . . . Out of sight, out of mind. . . . I'm only interested in what I am doing now." That's my attitude, too.

MY FATHER, who was a church-going, nine-to-five guy—did his best to raise me on my own after my mother died. My aunt who lived right behind us helped to raise me, too. My father also had a housekeeper named Miss Sanoni—she was from the Deep South—and she would come over every day and cook these Southern dishes for dinner. So they all chipped in to raise me.

Well, *raise* me? That's kind of a stretch. Wasn't too much *raising* going on. Just like my mother, my father wasn't much of a talker. He was more of a supporter. The bills were paid. I ate. Nurturing? Naw.

That wasn't my pops' style. Nobody in my immediate circle talked to me much. Nobody asked about how I was feeling. That's the main reason that, these days, I *talk* to my kids a lot. I *talk* to my wife a lot. But in my house as a kid, there was just not a lot of conversation. My parents and my aunts weren't made in that let's-talk-it-out mold.

You'd expect a boy who lost his mother to start wilding out, turn into a real menace. But I never got into too much mischief, except for this one situation with my bike. The year after my mother passed, my father got me a bicycle for Christmas. So I rode it to show one of my friends and I put it on its kickstand in front of his house. I went inside to play with his racing cars. When I came back outside—fuck me—my bike was stolen.

At first I was scared to tell my father that my bike, my brand-new Christmas present, was stolen. And finally when I told him, he didn't raise his voice. He didn't raise his hand. He just shrugged.

"Well, then, you ain't got no bike."

And he went back to putting away the groceries. That was how matter-of-fact he was. Eventually I got this sneaky game going, learned how to boost pieces of bikes, a couple wheels here, a frame there, a seat, some handlebars. I never had the heart to steal a *whole* bike, so I just put the bits and pieces together. While my dad was still at work, I had a little chop shop going in my garage. And I put the stolen parts together of all these different bikes, learned to assemble them like a pro. It was kind of a Frankenbike, but I hooked it up nice with some spray paint and model paint. Then after I did one, it kind of got good to me. By the sixth grade, I got a pair of bolt-cutters and went out stealing parts of other bikes. I must have thought I was a real little criminal mastermind. I would sneak out of the house while my father was asleep, go out on the prowl at night, walk over to another neighborhood, and steal the parts I needed, hooking up my own bicycles.

My father never noticed that I went from having *no* Christmas bike to having three or four weird-looking, brightly painted bikes all around the yard and in the garage. Or if he did notice, he just never said shit to me about it.

As far as parenting styles go, my dad was a real old-school dude. One evening stands out in my mind. My father, Miss Sanoni, and I were at the kitchen table, finishing up dinner. My pops said something to me, and for some unknown reason, I decided I wanted to mumble something back. This was the first time in my life I tried to talk back to him and say something fly. I said it so quiet, I thought I got away with it. But when I stood up, my father stood up, too. I can still remember the way the legs of his chair screeched on the linoleum. He took one step toward me and he hit me square in the solar plexus. *Boom.* My knees buckled, and in slow motion I fell to the kitchen floor. Knocked all the breath out of me. Then he stood over me.

"Boy, you talk shit to me when you can *whoop* me."

That's the way it was done. He didn't give me a spanking or a slap in the face. He hit me like a grown man. He was putting me in check, trying to show me what happens to men in the real world when they talk shit.

You see a lot of people on the Internet talking mad shit, because if they did the same thing in a room full of people there would be repercussions. If that was a face-to-face conversation, somebody would step to them, hit them in the solar plexus, and have them doubled-up on the ground.

When you come from an environment where people have no problem putting you in check physically, you learn you better measure your words. Be careful what the fuck you say. My dad was teaching me a real valuable lesson, one I never forgot: Never mumble some sarcastic shit to somebody who *obviously* can fuck you up.

I WASN'T *LONELY.* But I felt pretty alone after my mother died. Then, when I was in the seventh grade, I found myself *truly* alone.

For me it was just a regular day at Summit Junior High. I was twelve years old, and I'll never forget that spring morning, getting pulled out of class and taken down to the principal's office. The principal's face was pale, and he kept mumbling something about how sorry he was, how sorry. I stood there in silence. *Sorry about what?* And there was this *look* on both the principal's and the secretary's faces. I now understand that look. It's the look of a person trying to tell you—but they can't find the words—that somebody died. Man, that's an *ill* look.

The principal told me, "Tracy, you need to go home now. Something terrible has happened."

That word hung in the silence of the office. I mean when you're twelve years old, that word *terrible* does nothing but amplify the fear and anxiety about whatever's coming at you.

I left the office. I don't remember getting into a car, but somebody must've driven me to my aunt's house. My aunt, whose eyes looked swollen, told me what happened.

"Tracy, your dad just passed."

Both of my parents died really young—still in their thirties—of massive heart failure, four years apart. I was still so young that the experiences of both of my parents' deaths are kind of blurred together in my mind. And being an only child, I was going through all of it in my own little bubble.

The first thing that happens is you get shuttled off into this place where everyone is trying to protect you. The wake and funeral is happening, and you can see all the adults getting dressed in black, and preparing the flowers. But they keep you away, sheltering you from the reality of death. All these grown folks are wailing and sniffling, but they try to hide it from you, since you're a kid. All day long, these older people are coming at you, saying, "Tracy, are you okay?"

"Yeah, I'm all right."

"Are you *sure* you're okay?"

"Yeah."

Here's what's real strange. Everybody—all the adults around me, I mean—expected me to be losing my shit. Just trippin'. And not only was I *not* trippin', I was not even *engaged* in it. It was almost like I had the ability to will myself into this zone where it really didn't seem to be happening to me. I was emotionally about a million miles away from all the adults, all the crying and the handkerchiefs, and I just had one thought in my mind:

So what's next? What's the next move?

Yeah, I was detached. But looking back on my childhood, I don't think there was an *attachment*. In other words, even when I was a little kid and I'd fall off my bike, skin my knees and want to cry, there was nobody to really cry to. So I learned to suck it up really quick. I'd hit the ground, dust my ass off and not show anybody that I was fucked up. I wasn't one of these kids who was always coming home with hurt feelings, running to hug my mother. None of that clingy, emotional shit was my reality. I grew up in a nonaffectionate household. I think kids are trained to know what they're going to get, and once they get a taste of it, they'll always want more. It's like that shit with Pavlov's dog. If you cuddle a kid a lot, he'll want more cuddling. If you don't, he'll just accept that as his reality. He doesn't look for the added affection.

Everybody in the family was bugging out that I didn't cry when my father died. They remembered how I hadn't shed a tear for my mother, either. But I just wasn't built like that. Wasn't wired like that. I didn't have an ounce of self-pity in my bones. It didn't hit me, *Damn, I'm an orphan.* Even as a twelve-year-old kid, I *knew* I was going to have to make it on my own, and my survival instincts were kicking in.

"WHETHER HARDCORE OR NOT
YOU WORE THE RIGHT COLOR
OR YOUR ASS GOT SHOT . . ."
—**"THAT'S HOW I'M LIVIN'"**

2.

I DIDN'T HAVE A LOT of family, which meant I didn't have a lot of options. Like I said, my mother had *no* relatives that we knew; my father had two sisters, and for a few months I lived with my aunt who lived right behind our duplex, but then I was sent to my other aunt and her husband in Los Angeles—supposedly just for the summer.

One afternoon, a few weeks into the summer, a delivery truck with all these boxes arrived—my clothes from the house in New Jersey. Shit, it was disorienting. Nobody even took the time to explain what was happening. I didn't know my aunt and her family; they were essentially strangers to me. And what made it tense was the fact that my aunt had already raised two kids; her youngest, my first cousin Earl, had just graduated from high school, so my aunt and uncle were in that mode to retire, be empty nesters, get on with that next stage of their lives.

And *now* here comes this kid from Jersey. And not just any kid—an orphan, an adolescent, a boy just entering the wild-the-fuck-out years. Yeah, I felt a lot of resentment from them about me being there. Nobody said it outright, of course, but the vibe was always, *Okay—Tracy, we got to take care of you.* Never: *We want to take care of you.*

I was in limbo. Being relocated, when you're not expecting it, is some crazy shit. Even if you don't miss the kids you grew up with, you miss your routine, your habits, the way you know all the shortcuts and the back alleys when you're bombing around on your bike. Now you're in an absolutely foreign place. As foreign to you as Algeria or Argentina. You realize that you're back at square one. You realize that you don't know shit.

And I was about to find out the hard way that not knowing shit can be a life-or-death proposition for a teenager growing up in South Central L.A.

FORTUNATELY, I DIDN'T GET THROWN *straight* into the gladiator pits. I caught a break in that respect. My aunt lived in a middle-class black neighborhood, View Park. And the first school I went to in L.A. was Palms Junior High—a predominantly white school in Culver City. They bused the black kids there, part of the court-mandated integration at the time in L.A. But it wasn't just the middle-class black kids like me coming into this white neighborhood; that was the first time I encountered kids that were coming on buses from South Central. They were tough in a way I'd never encountered, not actually gang members yet, but they were the younger brothers of cats who were definitely banging.

Going to a mostly white junior high in L.A., that was a different zone. Because now you're getting bused in with all the black kids, and you've got the little white girls every morning, already out in front of the school checking you out. And it's the height of puberty, so everybody's hormones are out of control. That's where the racial shit starts kicking in. Not some stupid, unspoken rule about all black kids going home when it gets dark. This was a lot more dangerous, because this was *sexual.* I'm going to tell it to you straight—I don't give a fuck. Little white girls are *intrigued* by little black boys. You ain't never going to shake that. And that leads to some of the biggest problems in the world, at least as far as the racists see it.

Maybe we had a little bit more swagger or whatever, but from the moment we got off the bus, the white girls thought we were the hottest shit going. That caused some drama. Because if you had a white girl-friend at Palms Junior High, you still had to get back on the bus and deal with the *sisters*. The white girls lived in Culver City, right by the school, but when the school day ended your ass was going back to the 'hood. And in junior high, your relationships are solely based at school. No one goes home to hang out at each other's house. The sisters used to give the brothers an earful about talking to them white chicks. I didn't have any girlfriends in junior high—I wasn't cool enough yet. But I was seeing a lot of my homeys dealing with all that drama.

The biggest trip to me with L.A. was the *size*. The city is so sprawl-ing, so spread out. It wasn't like the neighborhoods I was familiar with back East where there's twenty-five or thirty houses on the block. In some parts of L.A., your closest friend could be a five-minute drive away.

The first kid my age I met in View Park was Billy Arnold—years later he got killed in a terrible motorcycle accident. He was one of the coolest cats I ever met in my life. Billy had that kind of cool that's just inborn. I mean, this kid even had a cool Moms. He had a swagger, he had the flyest clothes and records; he even had a bedroom that looked like a seventies bachelor pad.

When I was getting sized up by the kids in the neighborhood—as a new-jack, don't matter where, you're always gonna get tested—Billy for some reason said he had my back. And because I was friends with this cool-ass kid, I was more or less connected. Across the street from Billy lived the Staintons, and one of the brothers was a black belt, so nobody even thought about fucking with them. Between Billy Arnold and the Stainton brothers I never really had problems with bullies or assholes trying to mess with me.

During junior high, we were still protected from the whole gang thing. Even though kids from gang-affiliated neighborhoods were get-ting bused to Palms, back in the seventies when I was in the eighth grade the gang situation was just starting in earnest. But I was about to get a crash course in the gangster life in high school.

AFTER GRADUATING FROM JUNIOR HIGH, I decided I wanted to go to a local high school, Crenshaw High, which was walking distance from my aunt's home. I was sick of the busing bullshit.

From the jump, my head was spinning. Number one, it was an almost 100 percent black school. Wasn't one white kid there. And just one Mexican. L.A. is fucking segregated like that.

All these kids coming from inner-city junior highs to Crenshaw already got their little cliques. There were a total of four guys that went to Palms that came to Crenshaw, including my boys Franzell and Burnett, so I didn't have a crew. I wasn't really connected. My homey Sean E. Sean—folks got to know him later in my records and videos—was a grade below me, so he was still at Palms when I started Crenshaw.

I felt like I was walking into a prison yard by myself. Hell yeah, it was intimidating. Plus, I was a tiny ninth grader, and there were eighteen-year-old twelfth graders. These dudes were big—looked like grown-ass 225-pound men with sideburns and a five o'clock shadow at noon.

When I hit Crenshaw High, the gang situation started to heat up in the L.A. school system. You have to understand—gangbanging started from a very small area in South Central L.A. The Crips and Bloods started in a handful of blocks, and it took a while for it to branch out through all the schools in a city as big as Los Angeles. It started down at Washington High. Washington, Jordan, Jeff, Freemont. Those were the ground-zero high schools where the gangs were coalescing. And by that summer, the gang life was just hitting Crenshaw. In its own way, Crenshaw was a crucial location, because it was the school that was the unofficial dividing line between the East Side and the West Side.

The dividing line between East and West is Crenshaw Boulevard. Technically the dividing line is the Harbor Freeway—that's in gang terms—but in school terms, the line is drawn at Crenshaw Boulevard. After you go to the other side of Crenshaw, you get to Westchester, Palisades, University, L.A. High, Fairfax—those are all West Side schools. The middle-ground schools are Crenshaw and Manual Arts—right down the middle of the East–West divide.

There were subtle distinctions, but they meant a lot to kids. The

West Side kids were always known to be a little bit slicker, have a little bit more money, dress a little bit more fly. The East Side kids were tougher, wilder, more aggressive. Straight up—I understand it now—they were just the poorer kids. We used to say that the girls on the West Side looked better, too—again, it's just money; they could afford to have nicer clothes and gear. Also, as you moved more to the West Side, you'd get more into the interracial dating, so you'd see more and more mixed-looking kids. We had the lighter-skinned black girls on the West Side. And we thought that was something to be proud of.

Because Crenshaw was a borderline school, there was still a mixing of the sets, and you had Bloods and Crips in the halls at the same time. That led to serious drama. Constant beefing. I remember at one point *Time* magazine referred to us as *Fort* Crenshaw.

Nobody schooled me about the colors. That was an unwritten code that ran deep. And you didn't have a lot of time to decipher it. You'd see cats with pressed khakis, bomber jackets from the Army surplus store. They rocked Levis, but in their own distinctive way. Always cuffed on the outside. Some of the neighborhood O.G.'s would go for this Prohibition Era–look, rocking pinstriped vests and a kind of fedora called the ace-deuce. The ace-deuces look almost like derbies, but they've got a micro-brim around them, really small and tight to the head. Cats would take hairnets and pull them over the top of the ace-deuce. They'd wear suspenders, but they'd let them droop down around the waist, not tight over their shoulders. Crips were known for their crocus-sack shoes, always in shades of blue, brown, or black. That was a gangster staple. And, of course, there was the flag. The blue bandanna had to be folded precisely in the left back pocket.

Crenshaw High was run by the Hoover Crips. When I started at Crenshaw, the biggest gang rivalry was with the Brims. Crips and Brims. The Brims wore red and Crips wore blue. The Crips kept their rag in the left pocket; the Crips pierced their left ear. The Brims did everything on the right. Like a mirror image.

The Crips had all these different divisions and sets: Eight-Trey Gangsters, the Hoovers, the Harlem Crips. Every other gang united *against* the Crips, and any gang that wasn't Crip by default became

Brim. The Van Ness Boys, the Denver Lanes, the Pirus, the Inglewood Family, the Athens Park Boys, all of them united into a coalition—over time the Brims came to be known as the Bloods.

When I first got to Crenshaw that summer, there was still a gang in effect called the Bishops—a Brims gang. Over time, during my years at Crenshaw, all the Brims started to go to Manual Arts, and Dorsey. The Crips took over Crenshaw. Anyone who wasn't a Crip, or from a Crip neighborhood, would transfer out.

IT DIDN'T TAKE LONG for me to learn how to walk the walk. In South Central, it's called survival. You had to know to wear your blue and look a certain way or else deal with the consequences. Shit runs so much deeper than just not wearing red. You had to learn which neighborhoods were sworn enemies. Over time there were these major wars between rival sets of Crips, like the Rollin' '60s and the Eight-Trey Gangsters—Monster Kody's set—and cats kept on gunning down each other for decades. With those dudes, the banging became generational—younger brothers and cousins taking revenge on murdered family—like vendettas in the Mafia.

You had to know to call your people "cuz" and never "blood." Just saying, "S'up, blood?"—something I used to hear older dudes say all the time back in New Jersey—could get you gunned down quick.

On most blocks in South Central, there really are no neutrals. Everyone's forced under the jurisdiction of the gangs just to stay out of the drama. You might show up in South Central a clean-cut, square kid—like I did—but before you know it, you got the blue or red bandanna folded up perfectly in your left or right back pocket. Everyone learns the rules fast. Even the girls. Eventually, if you went anyplace in town and said, "I go to Crenshaw," people would consider you a Crip by affiliation.

You might try to tell them, "But I ain't in no gang."

"Naw, nigga. You from Crenshaw. You a Crip. You *know* them niggas."

"No, I don't."

"Shut the fuck up. You know 'em. And we gonna send them a message through you."

And that's the trip. In the gangbanging world, you can get it just for knowing motherfuckers. It's murder by affiliation.

WHEN I STARTED AT CRENSHAW, the most feared shot caller in L.A. was Stanley "Tookie" Williams. Of course, years later Tookie became nationally known while he was on death row—considered a stone-cold murderer by some; admired as a rehabilitated anti-gang activist and author by others. Tookie wasn't the founder of the Crips—that was Raymond Washington—but Took became the undisputed leader of all the West Side Crips. From time to time, Tookie and his crime partner, Jimel Barnes from the Avalon Gardens Crips, used to roll through Crenshaw.

They were both huge, hardcore bodybuilders and, throughout South Central, they were treated like rock stars. Back then, gangbanging was based on lifting weights. Wasn't all this gunplay shit. And you better believe Tookie was *serious* about his weight game. Tookie looked like he could take away Arnold Schwarzenegger's title. When you saw Tookie in real life, you felt like you were ten years old and he was forty. It's like, "These are some grown-ass men." You didn't even want to make eye contact with them.

All the original hardcore bangers were diesel, and that's where a lot of the gangster posturing originated. Back then dudes would fight. Back then you had to have hand skills. Wasn't nobody shooting nobody over the dumb, petty shit like they do nowadays. It wasn't based on that. Back then you had actual tough guys. Not everybody was a muscle-bound monster; there was always some little guys in the clique, but trust me, they could fight, too.

Tookie and Jimel looked almost like twins, except that Jimel was light-skinned and Tookie was darker. Most days, they dressed identically in farmer overalls with the bib down, showing off their bare chests, shoulders, and arms. They'd pull up at house parties in a low-rider, and actually had some younger Crips in their set—walking beside them, rubbing baby oil on their muscles so they could pose, flex, and have all these sixteen- and seventeen-year-old girls swarming them, screaming, going crazy.

Tookie wasn't a regular presence at Crenshaw, but I was in homeroom with some of the most feared Crips of the time. Cats like Babyface. Anthony Hatchett. Jaw Bone. These were legendary banger names.

One time this banger from Van Ness Boys, a feared Brim named Butch, showed up unannounced and just mobbed through the school. He came through Crenshaw on some one-man-army shit. The high-ranking Crip bangers weren't around that day. Butch didn't fuck anybody up; he just walked around, posturing, threw his set up, talking mad shit.

The next day when the real bad-ass Crips got to Crenshaw, that's when it got violent. They started smacking niggas up.

"Yo, Butch was up in this muthafucka? What the fuck?"

They were pissed that we didn't defend our turf. But Butchie was big. Butchie looked like he could rep three hundred easily on the bench. We wasn't doing nothing to him. We just gave him a wide berth and hoped he'd leave quietly. . . .

Another time—before all the Brims transferred out of Crenshaw—I had a run-in with a Van Ness Boy named Gary. We were all in the school weight room. I'm trying to get buff, trying to get some weight on. I'm kind of standing off to one side, waiting for Gary to finish using the flat bench.

Gary wasn't quite as big as Tookie—but he was still one of the most jacked-up and scary-looking dudes you ever want to see. I didn't know who he was, didn't know his rep with the Brims. He was big as fuck, sure, but I didn't know this dude as a notorious banger.

For some reason, my stupid ass, while he's on the bench—a whole mess of forty-five-pound plates rattling—I get this uncontrollable urge to make a loud fart sound with my mouth, as soon as he lowers the bar to his chest and goes to press it.

I don't know what the fuck I was thinking.

Gary locks out the bar, racks the weights, sits up real slow, then looks at me.

He's real quiet at first: "Oh, you think that's funny?"

Now, I got this swoll-up 260-pound killer glaring at me.

"Nigga, come here!"

He takes me into this little area, between the gym and locker room. There was a short hallway, and he closed the door, locked me in there with him.

Then Gary tells me to hit him as hard as I can in the chest.

Now, at the time I'm maybe 130 pounds soaking wet. Gary is a wall of muscle, easily twice my weight. I'm scared to hit him, 'cause I think he's just using it as an excuse to kill me.

"Yo, just hit me, nigga!"

Finally, I hit him in the chest as hard as I could. It was like punching a truck. He didn't even flinch.

Then—*bam*—he dipped down and threw a short right hook into my leg.

Then he smiled. Then turned. And he bounced.

Talk about a fucking charley horse. I was doubled over. I could hardly walk.

Okay, Gary was too big to be fucking with me, but he had to teach me a lesson. If he'd hit me in the face, or broke my arm, he wouldn't have been respected for that. I was too small, and I wasn't gangbanging. It was just like, "The little homey did something stupid," and he checked me.

You saw a lot of that shit back in the day. Homeys getting checked by the older niggas.

About five minutes after, I was sitting in the locker room, nursing the charley horse. A bunch of my homeys crowded around me, breathless, shouting:

"Yo, fool! You know who you was fuckin' with?"

That shit left a bruise for a month.

YOU HAVE TO REMEMBER, I had never seen *nothing* back East. I didn't know anything about banging. I was green to all kinds of violence. It wasn't like I was from Brooklyn or the Bronx. It wasn't like I was from Newark—though I was technically born there. I was from Summit, and that's not a place where a kid would see gunplay or nothing. That's why I always claim the West Coast. I didn't kick up any dust back East. I was a late-bloomer in this criminal game.

Gangs have transformed radically since my day. Once crack hit, it changed the whole gang system from being territorial and about neighborhood pride into sheer free enterprise, straight crime-for-hire. There's not any real-true pecking order anymore. Today it's strictly about money. Back then, I don't even think the gangs *made* money. It was about reppin' your block, reppin' your hood, reppin' your set.

In the eighties and nineties, the crack game broke all the gangs and splintered them off into little money-making sets. It made everything more violent, more about gunplay, more about constant retaliation. That's when most people across the country started hearing about the Crips and Bloods, when there was already a bloodbath in L.A.

Honestly, I don't think gangbanging could have taken off the way it had if it had started off so violent. That life had to get a foothold, almost based on teams. Based on neighborhood camaraderie. Dudes were still scary, but they still had some codes of chivalry, still had more innocent shit like Gary checking me without really doing serious damage.

The irony is, the more violent the life got, the more inescapable it got. Once people started to die all the time, that's when cats could no longer get out. Because when murder is added into the mix, banging transforms into a whole other thing. It's not like you can quit your set now.

I was lucky in the sense that I never got formally inducted into the gangbanging. I was never jumped into a set. And the only reason is because I didn't live in the 'hood with the gang. I was still walking to school from my block in View Park. My friends, Burnett and Franzell, and I were coming down from the hills, and we actually created a gang, more or less as a joke, called the EPA—Eliminators Pimpin' Association. It started as a laugh, but it escalated, until we basically had Crenshaw niggas believing that there was a hundred muthafuckas in the hills. We set up our own thing, but it was like a shell company. It was just the three of us in the whole fucking gang.

Still, my boy Burnett was a big, tough guy, and Franzell was a guy who'd moved from the Avenues into the hills. He had that street swagger, being an Avenues kid. His mother was actually a Crip Mama—that's a mother that deals day-to-day with the gangs. So having a couple of tough friends, that's all it took. We never got punked.

Outsiders don't always know this, but you can't join a set if you're not from that neighborhood. It was only toward the end of my time at Crenshaw that I really got closer to the gang life. When I got into the twelfth grade my girlfriend, Adrienne, was in the tenth grade. She was a light-skinned girl, athletic build, with a crazy body, big booty—just my type. Somehow or other I found the right words to talk to her. We hooked up and it was a while before I realized that she lived in the heart of Hoover hood—73rd and Hoover. I ended up getting affiliated with their set, because I started to go over there and hang out with the Hoover Crips.*

See, that's how it works in the street. My girl's a Criplette, so I'm brought in and I'm affiliated. The act of actually banging is different: It's retaliating, doing drive-bys, and all that shit is like being a frontline soldier. Now, if you live in the neighborhood, you're going to wear the colors—you damn sure can't wear the other colors—and you become an affiliate. And if you're dating a girl from the neighborhood, you get that same affiliation. *Oh, we know Trey. Trey's good with us. Come shoot craps, come party, come hang out.* You're part of the set, but it would be disrespectful and dishonest to claim you're an actual banger.

They liked my style, I was a little flyer, I had that West Side look. I got a cool personality. I've always had a sucker-proof personality. If people get past the surface and get to know me, within thirty minutes I can flip pretty much anybody. I'm not trying to sound boastful. I'm just a cool dude—or try to be.

I met Adrienne's brother and younger sister; I met everybody on her block. The gangbangers on the block took to me.

I was a lightweight, but starting to become a hustler. I could gamble. I could talk the talk. I was slick. I didn't let anyone call me "Tracy"

---

* These days the Hoovers have broken away from the Crips and call themselves ABK—Any Body Killers. They're now known for combining the color orange with the blue, wearing orange bandannas in their back pockets and Houston Astros baseball caps with a prominent orange *H*.

anymore—that sounded like a girl's name to me. I was known in the streets as "Trey."

One of the shot callers from the 'hood was a guy everyone called Puppet, he was the real Hoover O.G. For some reason, he took me under his wing. I used to sit up in Puppet's house, he'd be saying, "Yo Trey, maybe we should roll on these Swans."

He was setting up drive-bys with me sitting right next to him. "Yo, Trey. We should blast these niggas."

I was thinking, *Hold up, Cuz. That ain't what I do! You niggas wanna do war talk, I'm over here chilling with my girlfriend, while you bangers are plotting out shit.*

Still, I was deep enough in the life to understand one crucial thing about the gang life: The flip side of the violence and negativity is the love. And that's some extreme love. Extreme love.

I only realized this recently: When I got to Crenshaw High, that's the first time I'd ever heard someone say *love* to me.

My aunt never said she loved me. My mother and father were never big on that word.

You get to Crenshaw, and you got a male friend saying, "Cuz, ain't nothin' never fin' to happen to you, homey. You safe, cuz. I *love* you."

That's some heavy shit. Like a lot of the homeys, I was getting something I wished I'd gotten from my father. When I was a little kid and something happened to me, I didn't want my dad to call the police. Fuck that. I wanted to say, "Go get 'em, Dad!" Of course, hardly anybody has it like that in real life, but every little kid wants to *believe* that his pops is Superman.

And that protection you get from the gang is something most people in the 'hood don't get from their families. To me, it's interesting that some of the kids who came from big families, families with four or five brothers, didn't need to join the gangs. Because they had that unconditional protection. "Yo, don't fuck with me—I got a couple of brothers that will come *see* you, nigga." I didn't have that big family structure. And like everybody else, I wanted that feeling that someone had my back.

Yes, the first I really heard love expressed was with the Crips. Not only heard the word "love," but saw it firsthand. Saw it manifested. Saw

that if you fuck with one of us, you fuck with *all* of us. That's very en-
ticing. That's very attractive to a young brother.

It's human nature. We've always had armies and tribes, teams and
squads. That sense of loyalty, brotherhood, love—it's very primal, it's at
the core of what it means to be a human. And it's authentic love—as
real and as deeply felt as any love out there—but it's just misdirected in
gangs.

3.

I COULDN'T STAND LIVING with my aunt. Maybe it was the fact that I was dressing the part of a Crip—flying my blue flag in her house—but we were beefing constantly. I've held my tongue for years, but my aunt's deceased now, so I can tell it like it was. She was the worst kind of hypocrite. She was a social worker *and* an alcoholic. So add that up. She was the person who, during the day, would check whether foster kids should be allowed to live in certain houses; but then, at night, she'd come home to her own house and drink half a gallon of liquor.

It wasn't a good place for me. Wasn't like I was in a *family.* I was in a boarding house. I was in a foster home, even though they were my real flesh-and-blood relatives. They didn't show any love at all.

Since I was an orphan—and still a minor—I was getting a Social Security check for $225 every month. My aunt and I had this one major blow-up when I was seventeen, and I said, "Look, just gimme my goddamn check and I'm *out!*" I'd been signing them over to her, but now I took that little Social Security money and bounced, found my own crib on Kansas Avenue. For the rest of my twelfth grade at Crenshaw, I was one of the coolest kids in school, because I had my own apartment for ninety bucks a month in the 'hood. People hung with me so much, motherfuckers used to run away from home to stay at my house for three or four days. My crib became a de facto drop-in center for the whole crew.

I didn't have any big ambitions. I guess I planned on being a workingman like my father. When I graduated from Crenshaw, I went to Trade-Tech College for half a year because I wanted to get a job doing auto body and fender repairs.

I was living on that $225 a month Social Security. My friends were hitting petty crimes, shooting dice, stealing car stereos, little bullshit, going in the direction of one day becoming big-time criminals. The writing was already on the wall.

I never got those gang tats everyone else was getting. The only thing I did was pierce my left ear. That was because of the kids I was hanging around with—and since the crowd was 99.9 percent Crips that was the only ear I could pierce. I didn't go to some shop in the mall. I got my ear pierced the old-school way, with a needle and a potato and some thread. Hurt like shit.

The one thing that separated me from most of my friends is that I never drank, smoked, or did drugs. It wasn't a moral decision. Like I said, my survival instincts kicked in real early. I was still half a child and I was sleeping alone in my own house. I was sitting around—a lot—alone. My friends weren't around *all* the time. So they'd come over and party, then leave, and I'd be sitting there just looking at the walls.

My mind went into this zone. In my mind, I called myself a "spot." Meaning if you looked at a crowd from the roof of a football stadium each person would be a spot—one tiny speck—and nobody gives a fuck about a spot. A spot is just one solitary life. If one of those spots, one of those people, comes up missing—who gives a shit? The stadium is still full. An anonymous speck. You don't mean shit. Even now—I've achieved some things, and got my share of money and fame—but if I died today, I'm not kidding myself, New York keeps moving.

I realized really young that my survival was all about me maintaining composure. At the end of the day, my survival was really only important to *me.*

I would look at people getting tore up, I'd seen my aunt hitting the booze hard, and I never thought it was attractive. I never thought being drunk was cool. And it didn't hurt that I couldn't stand the taste of liquor. Now, if there was a way to get drunk off some Kool-Aid, I'd probably have been an alcoholic!

I didn't have a problem with my boys being weed smokers. When I was selling it, you know, one of the first rules of the game is: Never get high on your own supply. My homeys would smoke around me; I had no problem with that. I'm not like my wife, Coco, who is literally allergic to weed, you can't even puff a toke within forty feet of her. But no, my boys smoked so much that I definitely caught contact highs. It didn't bother me. Just like I hated the taste of booze, I never smoked cigarettes, so taking something to my mouth and sucking the smoke in never made sense. It just seemed nasty.

But the main reason I never felt the need to make myself high was that I never felt the need to lose control. If I was drunk, I was vulnerable. If I was high, somebody could beat me out of something. I didn't have bodyguards, I didn't have brothers, didn't have family. I didn't have anybody. If I hit the floor, I would stay there—*forever.*

And in South Central, that shit wasn't theoretical. Plenty of times I'd seen cats get taken advantage of when they were drunk and high.

Sure there was that peer-pressure bullshit.

When I was young, like in the tenth grade, dudes would try to push it on me.

"Yo, Trey! Hit the weed."

"Naw, I don't want to hit the weed."

"Well, if you don't hit the weed, then you's a bitch."

"Well if I'm a bitch, why don't you *make* me hit the weed?"

The thing about peer pressure is once you say "No" enough times, even the motherfucker who's most adamantly trying to get you to smoke can become your biggest supporter. See, long before the term "designated driver" came into use, motherfuckers in the hood realized how valuable it was to have a sober homey. If the cops pulled us over, I could do the talking. If we went to party, there was at least one sober head in the house that knows to check that everybody is okay.

You take over the command position by default. Because you *ain't* high. You might have another guy in the clique that's more prominent, got more of that alpha male streak to him, but you're the one grabbing his ass to protect him when shit's going down. So often in the hood, the sober man has the most power. I liked that. I liked being in control, liked having that command spot. I took pride in not being high. I took pride in that leadership role it gave me.

I WAS KEEPING ON A straight path as far as the drinking and drugging went, but then that first semester of Trade-Tech, in 1976, I got my girlfriend Adrienne pregnant. I was so inexperienced with sex, I was literally ignorant. I didn't understand birth control. To be honest, this wasn't my thousandth nut—I was still green, and hadn't had a lot of sex. Nobody I knew had condoms; we thought you had to go to a doctor's office to get condoms.

I was afraid of being a teenage father, but in a stupid way, I wanted to have the kid because at that point I was zeroed out, I didn't have any family. I thought it would be a good thing to have a child. At the same time, Adrienne's parents weren't crazy about her having a kid in the tenth grade. I convinced her to have the baby. Kind of ironic, because usually guys in that situation are saying, "No, don't. I can't handle the responsibility." That wasn't my thing. I was saying, "Let's do it! Let's have this baby!" while her parents were trying to get her to have it "taken care of." And we were both so naïve, we didn't even understand what abortions were at that point.

Adrienne went along with me and had the baby girl, who we named LeTesha. We struggled. Adrienne was still going to high school and I took care of the baby. I had no job but still had to come up with the money for food, clothes, and diapers. I started doing anything I could to bring in some bucks. Little petty crimes. Boosting car stereos. Even selling bags of weed like my homey Sean E. Sean. But the petty crime wasn't cutting it.

This was a moment in life when I didn't know what I was going to do, but I knew I had to do *something*. When my daughter came home from the hospital, my girl and I were all crowded into a little apartment, getting up with the baby all night—I didn't feel like I had a future.

One morning, as I was running on no sleep due to a colicky baby, something came over me. I started thinking about this enlistment office on Crenshaw Boulevard. It was right nearby. I used to walk past it nearly every day.

I walked over there, full of swagger and testosterone. Came in the door and made straight for the recruiter.

"Yo, I want to be in the army," I said.

When I sat down to take the test, I scored pretty high. I could have had my pick of branches—Army, Navy, or Air Force. At the time, I was kind of a jock. I'd been on the gymnastics team at Crenshaw. I hardly ever tell people I was on the Crenshaw gymnastics team—because we *sucked.* Still, I learned to do the pommel horse, parallel bars, and rings. That shit takes a lot of stamina, upper body and core strength. So at eighteen years old, I was in top physical shape, and I figured I'd go infantry.

My plan was to become Ranger-certified, and then get assigned to the 25th Infantry Division out in Hawaii, Schofield Barracks—I'd heard some of the old-time cats in South Central talking about the famous Tropic Lightning outfit, which had some history and glory. I signed up to be a paratrooper—you got an extra $2,500 bonus pay for being Airborne—which sounded exciting as hell to me. At the recruiting office, they told me I could be Airborne stationed at Schofield Barracks.

But first, I had to do six weeks of basic training at Fort Leonardwood, Missouri. We called it Fort Lost-in-the-Woods in the State of Misery. That's some of the wildest shit you'll ever do—once you get off that cattle truck, and the sergeants start screaming, you begin to have doubts, you really question yourself. *What the fuck did I just get myself into?* But you tough it out. You get through basic by telling yourself it's survival of the fittest.

After basic, you get shipped out to Advanced Infantry Training in Fort Benning, Georgia. It was while I was doing my A.I.T. at Fort Benning that I got a lesson in how the military really works—not the recruiting poster bullshit about BE ALL THAT YOU CAN BE. It's funny to think about it now, but all through Advanced Infantry Training, me and a couple of other guys spent half our time *stealing* for our company. It was mostly supplies and gear, one big-ass flagpole—all this shit that the officers wanted and couldn't get for some reason through requisitioning. One of the commanding officers singled out a bunch of us guys who seemed to have some street smarts about us. I was basically the leader, and at night we would go out onto the post and boost the shit he wanted.

That little crime spree came to a head when he told us we had to go steal an infantry-blue rug for his office. We found the rug in the nearby guesthouse. We had to wait for the guest to leave, then we snuck in, rolled the rug up, and snatched it. But our dumb asses hadn't planned properly, and another officer, who was supposed to meet us with a Jeep, bitched out and never showed. So we were stuck carrying this big-ass rug. We hid it, and figured we'd come back the next day to get it. The first day it was reported missing, the rug was only about twenty-five yards from the guesthouse.

We went back, grabbed the rug, shoved it into a cab, and got it back to our unit. We delivered it to the CO, just like all the other stuff we'd stolen. Of course, the cabdriver went and snitched, and the next morning I got woken up by C.I.D., the Criminal Investigation Command of the military. They rounded all of us up, they cracked us, and they put us in the jail on the post.

But the insane part was—just to show you how fucked-up the military can be—while I was in jail, they gave me my $2,500 bonus. I mean, the bureaucracy of the military is so retarded, nobody checks with anybody else, so they ended up giving $2,500 to a dude in jail awaiting a military trial for burglary.

So I'm cooling my ass in jail, which is really just a converted barracks that they'd turned into a holding cell for soldiers awaiting trial.

But as soon as they handed me the bonus, I stared at the money. I stood up and told the other dudes, "Dig, I'm getting the fuck outta here."

The holding cell wasn't too secure. And it connected to an office. I

managed to work my way over into the office, got on a phone, and figured out when a civilian plane was leaving Columbus Airport. I timed
my escape to the airline schedule. I waited until there was just enough
time for me to make it from the post to the airport and buy a cash ticket
for the plane. The other two dudes who were locked up with me didn't
want to break out. They were scared.

"Naw, man, we ain't goin' AWOL."

We were locked in, of course, but it wasn't like we were in maximum
security. There were no bars on the windows. The top window wouldn't
go up, but I figured out a way to make the top window come down a
few inches. Just enough for a skinny dude to squeeze through. I went up
to the top bunk and managed to wriggle my ass out of the top window.
I had to time my escape so that the guards at the gates wouldn't see me.
It was just like breaking out of a prison.

In the lockup, we were all wearing distinctive prisoner's uniforms.
They were like standard-issue fatigues but they didn't have our name
patches—which was a dead giveaway to any MP looking for an es-
capee—so I had to creep back into my own barracks and grab one of my
uniform coats that had the name MARROW and all my insignia. I got
dressed and looked just like any other enlisted man on the post.

I flagged a cab, went to Columbus Airport, and paid cash for a
one-way ticket to L.A. Security at the airports wasn't as tight then as
it is these days, especially on domestic flights, so you could buy a
last-minute ticket with cash and—*boom*—you were sitting on the hot
tarmac, taxiing inside a California-bound Boeing.

A couple hours later I was back in Los Angeles, AWOL, and without a fucking plan. How long was that going to last? Couldn't go back
to my crib, because that's the first place the MPs would come look
for me.

So I stayed on the lam, ducking and dodging, hanging out at some of
my friends' houses. After a few weeks, I realized I had to call back to the
fort to squash this shit before I got hauled before a court martial looking to hammer me with some *real* prison time. I called the post and, finally, I got my CO who'd asked us to pull all the burglaries.

"Dig, I ain't fin' to go to jail for this shit," I told him.

He started to tell me he couldn't help, but I cut him the fuck off.

"You got a lot more to lose than me. You got your retirement on the line. So figure this shit out!" I said. "Call me when it's smoothed over, and I'll come back."

It was petty crime, wasn't like we were stealing guns or munitions, but it was still a burglary charge. None of us wanted that shit on our records. This CO was a lifer; he'd put twenty-plus years in the Army and he was getting ready to retire. So he had every motivation to squash the case.

I stayed AWOL, hiding out in L.A. for a month, and then I got a call saying it was all over. The stolen infantry-blue rug had been returned. I had to turn myself in to AWOL Apprehension in Long Beach. I wasn't considered a high-risk prisoner. Sometimes they handcuff you to an MP and put you on a plane, but they didn't categorize me as a flight risk so they just handed me a ticket and I returned to Fort Benning like it was nothing.

I did receive an Article 15, which is basically a military reprimand. But that was it. Slap on the wrist. They probably would have busted me down in rank, but I didn't have any rank to begin with, so they just sent me on to my post.

DESPITE THE ARTICLE 15, I managed to make it through Advanced Infantry Training. After Fort Benning, I went on to Advanced Individual Training. To become Airborne certified, I had to do a three-week course: Ground Week, Tower Week, and Jump Week. Ground Week, you're jumping off platforms, learning how to perform a PLF (parachute landing fall), which is critical in not busting your fucking legs when you hit the ground. Tower Week, you make jumps from a thirty-four-foot and two-hundred-fifty-foot tower—this funky old relic that had been trucked in from some World's Fair. All the students are in harnesses, jumping in succession—*boom, boom, boom*—learning how to make a mass exit.

Personally, I never had a fear of heights, but some cats who weren't fazed by the idea of jumping out of a chopper at more than a thousand feet *freaked* when they had to make the thirty-four-foot tower jump. For one thing you could actually see the ground up close. And on the tower, you're static, connected to a cable. So it's all psychological: in the back of your mind you still think you have the option to back out. Once you get into a C-130 there's no turning back. You got no option but to jump the fuck out.

If you make it through Ground and Tower Weeks, you graduate to Jump Week. You've got to make five acceptable jumps from an aircraft into the Fryar Drop Zone. Two were jumps with a rucksack and a dummy assault weapon. The other three jumps are called "Hollywood jumps," meaning you only wear your parachute and reserve. We jumped out of old planes like C-119s, C-130s, and C-141s. That was one of the best weeks of my Army career. I may not have done any drugs, but I was definitely an adrenaline fiend. I got more than my share of it at Jump School . . . I'll never forget the chant we used to do while we were about to make the jump.

> **Stand up, hook up, shuffle to the door, jump right out and count to four.**
> **If that chute don't open wide, I've got another one by my side:**
> **If *that* chute don't open, too, look out Devil I'm comin' through . . .**

When you get into your specialized training, you could become Airborne—depends on what base they send you to. If you get shipped to a full Ranger Battalion, you're going to be with nothing but Rangers.

But after completing Ranger training I found out something that had my brain in knots for days. I learned that you can't be Airborne and be stationed in Hawaii. There is no designated Rangers unit at Schofield Barracks. The recruiting officer on Crenshaw Boulevard had bullshitted me. So I terminated jump status and went to a straight-leg infantry. I didn't want to be stationed at Fort Bragg. I wanted to be at Schofield Barracks, out in the Pacific, with the surf and the sunshine and the girls. I joined the Army to support my baby daughter, but the biggest attraction was the opportunity to serve in Hawaii.

Eventually, I flew out to meet my unit, the 25th Infantry, Schofield Barracks, the Tropic Lightning outfit. It was a hell of a good posting. As far as weather and scenery goes, you couldn't find a better post in the entire U.S. military.

You're out there on the islands and there wasn't much to it except drilling in formation every morning, jumping in Jeeps, and doing war games in the fucking Kahuka Mountains. I learned to shoot an M2-03 grenade launcher. For a while I carried a 90mm recoilless rifle. I was an assistant gunner on an M60. I shot the TOW rocket, which sits on top of a Jeep. I shot the Dragon, which you need to carry. It's a wire-guided missile that shoots out of a missile launcher.

I enjoyed all that armaments training. Would have been *fun* if you could walk to it. If you could roll out of bed and stroll to it, it would've been a blast. But *nothing* in the military is designed to be fun. They make you march to everything and half the time they're screaming shit at you.

WHEN I LOOK BACK on my U.S. Army career, I always tell people, "I did two years in and two years out." Meaning, the first two years of my military stint I was gung ho, because I knew I was doing the right thing. I wanted to be the best goddamn M60 gunner on the base. I took pride in that shit. I felt I was giving my life direction.

But by the second year, I knew I didn't want to be a lifer. And I was just looking for a way to get out . . .

I'll never forget the turning point. I had a sergeant named Donovan who was a Ranger. You'd see lot of the old-timers with that Rangers patch on. These were guys who'd been in the military for decades, and were constantly changing their Military Occupational Specialty— MOS. Sergeant Donovan had seen combat in Vietnam.

Sergeant Donovan was always fucking with me. He fucked with a lot of the black infantrymen for a lot of reasons, but basically because we wouldn't cut our hair. We found a way to make our hair look regulation by packing it under our hats. It was just a little trick but that way, when we were on leave, we could comb our hair out and look like we were lo-cals. We found out really quick that you couldn't get any pussy if you were in the military. When you go off post, most of the girls in Hawaii, and especially the tourists, were warned not to fuck with the GIs from Schofield Barracks.

And these old sergeants like Donovan, I think their whole job de-scription was to make the enlisted men feel psychologically fucked up.

The hair issue really pissed Donovan off. He was always screaming, "You fuckin' losers—why don't you cut your hair?!"

And I didn't give a fuck really. I was used to him busting balls about my long hair packed up into my infantry hat.

I was a squad leader at Schofield Barracks. One morning I'm standing in formation with my squad, and Donovan decides to get about four inches from my grill. I could smell the stale coffee and Marlboros on his breath.

"Marrow!" he screamed. "You fucking loser! You're only here because you *can't make it* in civilian life."

You can't make it in civilian life. More than anything else, that's the one statement that propelled me to where I'm at today. I give Sergeant Donovan all the credit.

When he barked that shit in my face, I'm not gonna front: those words cut me deep. I'm standing there in formation, in the blazing tropical sun, and I'm looking at myself like some outsider would see me. And I said, *Damn, maybe it's the truth. What kind of future do I really have in the outside world?*

But that's the beautiful thing: Sometimes in life, someone will say something to you that either crushes you, breaks your spirit, or it drives you to the next level. After we broke ranks, I kept running over Donovan's words in my mind—*You can't make it, Marrow. You can't make it . . .*

ONE THING THAT HAPPENED during my time at Schofield Barracks was I got introduced to the pimpin' life. I'd met every kind of hustler at this point, cats who robbed banks, cats who sold coke, but this was my first close encounter with the real pimpin' game. One of my partners in the barracks, his girl had a sister who was a prostitute. So we used to hang out and get our weekend passes and go to her pimp's party. He was a fly-ass dude named Mac. He lived down by Diamondhead. Mac had it crackin' down there.

I'd been interested in the pimp game, but more from a distance. All through high school, I was reading Iceberg Slim. I picked up my street name, and later my rap name, from Iceberg Slim. He was the first author I discovered who truly delved into the life of crime and pimpin' and made it *real* to me. I went everywhere with his books, idolizing him. I'd memorized entire sections and could spit them at will. The Crips back in South Central used to constantly say, "Yo, kick some more of that shit by Ice, T."

And now I meet this real pimp in Hawaii. Mac liked the fact that I could quote Iceberg, and he started studying me at those parties. I was different from the other infantry dudes since I never drank or smoked. I mean, I partied and danced, but I was always detached from the shit. Mac used to pull me aside and talk to me. "Ice," he'd say. "Dig, you cut out for this here. You cut out for this pimpin' game. You got them light eyes. You don't seem to care about these girls."

But honestly, it always seemed a little too *obvious* to me. I always felt girls liked to flirt with you in order *not* to give you the pussy; they just liked to see men get weak. It wasn't sexual attraction; it was a mind-control thing.

But I was intrigued by the flashiness of the game. Over those months, Mac put me up to pimpin'—taught me the whole code. Mac was constantly telling me I was cut out to make a great pimp, but I also understood that this was part of his game: A pimp will tell you *whatever* he thinks you want to hear. That's what they do: They're masters and wizards of charisma. They'll make you feel good about everything they say. They'll compliment you until they work you into their world. So I listened. . . . And I smiled. . . . But I always kept Mac at arm's length.

In Hawaii prostitution seemed to be damn near legal. It's not exactly Nevada, but there are all these military bases—Schofield, Hickam, Shafter—and all this G.I. Joe testosterone running loose on the weekends. Plus, there are all these horny tourists coming into town daily. It's almost allowed by the cops, because they figure all these guys need to fuck something, or else there's going to be problems. So the hookers and the pimps are given a little space to flourish, almost like a safety valve, to keep all the dudes from killing each other.

AFTER SERGEANT DONOVAN GOT UP in my face with that shit, it was the dividing line. That's what made me determined to get out. I was *focused.* I wanted to prove to myself that I *could* make something of myself in the civilian world. Now came the tricky part. I was trying to get out, but I couldn't let on that I wanted out. I had a four-year stint to finish. If you let your superiors know you're looking to get out, damn straight, they'll bust you—take away your rank. I was just a PFC, but when they bust you down in rank, they're taking away your money. You have to ride it all the way out to the end. Then at the last minute, you say you want a discharge.

I was just going with the flow, keeping my plans a secret. So after that rah-rah first two years, I did my last two in the army, counting down the months. I was just saving enough money so I could take care of my daughter and maybe, after I got discharged, buy myself a Porsche. I still didn't know what I was going to do when I got out, but I got the idea of getting into the music scene, probably getting some gigs as a DJ in nightclubs. Maybe even promote a few parties. I was an infantryman in combat arms, so I wasn't trained for anything useful in civilian life. How are you supposed to put your expertise with the TOW rocket or as an M60 gunner down on a fucking job résumé?

Finally, when I was getting close to my discharge date, with about six months to go, I learned something that nobody had explained to me. A lot of bullshit in the military goes like that—you'll sign up to be a Ranger stationed at Schofield Barracks then find out months *after* all the training you can't fucking be a Ranger stationed at Schofield Barracks. And that's the way I learned about the "sole-parent discharge."

One night I pulled guard duty, which meant I'd be sitting at an ammo dump, which was *boring* as hell. I'd rather be digging drainage ditches than sitting on some fucking ammo dump all night. I tried to get out of it but couldn't.

For some reason, I was grumbling in the barracks about it: "Oh, you know, I couldn't get a babysitter. . . . Shit, now I got to move my kid. . . ."

And my CO overheard me and said, "What'd you say, Marrow?" "You got a *kid*? I didn't even know you had a kid." See, I never told anybody about my personal life off the base, so they didn't know I had a daughter.

"Yes sir, I've got a kid. I've got a baby daughter."

One thing led to another, and my CO explained it to me. Because I wasn't married, I was the main financial support for my daughter. And because I had no parents, no brothers, no sisters, the way the military looks at it, if something happens to me—if I get blown the fuck up in some training exercise in the mountains—my little baby girl is going to be on her own.

"Marrow," my CO said, "don't you know you can get out early? You could get out with an honorable right now. You're going to be getting out soon. But I'd advise you to take the discharge now, because in the next four months anything can happen to you."

Of course, when you're in the military, an honorable discharge is always the goal. But it's often like a moving target. There's a million ways they can void that contract, especially if they think you're not going to re-up. Anything can happen in your final few months. Since they were going to guarantee me an honorable discharge early as a sole parent, I jumped at the chance. I knew my CO was right. Who knew what shit might jump off in the final four months? I could wind up with a dishonorable discharge. Because of that offhanded remark I'd made trying to get out of guard duty, before I knew it, I was sitting down signing my early-discharge papers.

I managed to get an honorable, and four months ahead of schedule. And then I'm on a flight back home to L.A.

Little did I realize how much the game had changed since I'd left Crenshaw Boulevard.

PART TWO

NIGHTMARE WALKING

**"I SPEAK ON THIS WITH HESITATION
EVEN THOUGH WE'RE PAST
THE STATUTE OF LIMITATIONS."**
—"THAT'S HOW I'M LIVIN'"

4.

WHEN I HIT THE STREET in South Central, I barely recognized my old neighborhood. I checked in with my homeys and they told me the deal: The gangbanging had intensified. The firepower had escalated. Dudes were spraying their enemies with fully automatic weapons. Day-to-day life was constant murder and retaliation and more murder. It was nothing to be hanging on the corner and witness a drive-by where three or four bodies got dropped from the spray of an AK or an Uzi.

When I got home from the Army, I wanted to stay the fuck away from all that gangbanging and gunplay. While I was still in Hawaii, I'd been amassing all kinds of stereo equipment. At Schofield we could buy it from the PX dirt cheap. So I had two Technics turntables, a decent mixer, and some big speakers. My whole goal was to make a name for myself as a DJ. And the timing was good, because the L.A. club scene was thriving. There were production companies around L.A. who'd rent venues like the Veterans Auditorium and get a few thousand kids in the crowd. They'd take home a good chunk of cash. So I decided to make that my hustle. I started to get my gear and my flyers together to throw a few parties.

Meanwhile, during my four years away, the cats from my 'hood who'd been small-time criminals had started to make a mark for themselves. They were robbing jewelry stores, pulling daylight bank robberies. A younger brother of a homey from Crenshaw High set a record in California for the most banks ever robbed by a juvenile. All my closest homeboys, people like Sean E. Sean, Sean E. Mac, my man M.C., they'd all changed their game and were taking down jewelry stores. And it went from burglary to daytime bashes—what they call today "snatch and runs"—ultimately to gunpoint robbery.

Over a few months, my neighborhood created various teams of cats—squads made up of two guys and a girl—who'd enter a jewelry store and run diversion asking a bunch of distracting questions, while another member of the crew trimmed the jewelry case.

There was such a level of secrecy in my neighborhood. Certain cats were getting it. Other cats weren't getting it. You had to be admitted into that part of the clique. I was coming home from the Army, and even though I was down with the clique, I wasn't allowed to go on any jobs—we called them "licks"—right away.

But I had a friend named Nat the Cat. I kept bugging him about it. Finally, he told me how the shit worked.

"Listen," Nat said. "This is how it's going down. This is how we gettin' money."

Nat showed me the hustle of "trimming" a jewelry case, which was basically picking a lock. In those days, they used to have a special lock on jewelry cases called a pop-lock, and with nothing fancier than a nail file—we called that a "trim"—you could slide it into the lock and pop it. Clean and easy.

We called ourselves players—meaning nobody gets hurt. When we were finished robbing them, the store employees were dumbfounded. They didn't know what happened. A lot of times, a trim was done so slick, we didn't even have to run at the end. If it was done *real* smooth, the store wouldn't even notice until we were long gone.

But like everything else, the trimming started to escalate and became more aggressive. And I really didn't want to be in the drama. I just wanted to focus on making some kind of name for myself on the music scene.

DURING MY LAST YEAR in the military, not only had I learned to spin vinyl on my Technics, but that's when the Sugar Hill Gang dropped "Rapper's Delight." The record blew my mind. Not because rapping was something brand-new to me. Actually, the opposite: It blew my mind because I'd already been writing my own rhymes since high school. These weren't really raps, and we didn't know it as hip-hop. They were what we'd call Crip Rhymes. I can still reel off two or three of them at the drop of a dime.

Strollin' through the city in the middle of the night
Niggas on my left and niggas on my right
Yellin' *C-C-C-Crip* to every nigga I see
If you bad enough come fuck with me

I seen another nigga I said "Crip" again
He said, "Fuck a Crip nigga—this is Brim!"
So we pulled out the Roscoe
Roscoe said crack
I looked again nigga was shootin' back

So we fell to the ground aiming for his head
One more shot, nigga was dead
Walked over to him, took his gun
Spit in his face and began to run

So if you see another nigga laying dead in the street
In a puddle of blood from his head to his feet
I hope this time all you niggas get hip
That it's fuck a Brim, nigga—
This is *West Side* Crip!

I was saying this shit at Crenshaw back in '76, you dig? Which was way before I'd heard recorded rap. It was just something to do, these Crip raps, to entertain the set when we were chilling. It's a style that derives from hustlers toasting, putting their fly talk to rhyme; it's been part of the player code with guys like Iceberg Slim for ages. Iceberg did a record called *Reflections,* which had a lot of slick rhyming. Toasting and talking shit in verse is something that's always been a part of black culture—long before folks started calling it hip-hop—you can hear it in some old blues records, in some James Brown records, even the way Ali would boast in rhymes.

This was the same time that the early hip-hoppers were developing their styles in the Bronx, cats like Cold Crush, Busy Bee, Hollywood, Starski. But my rhyming wasn't connected to any kind of music. For me it was just a spoken-word style. All my boys would be sitting around, chilling, drinking, smoking weed.

"Yo, say one of your Crip rhymes, T."

These rhymes would be told among guys, but they weren't written to a beat. I never had a backing track, just a rhythm in my own head. When I heard "Rappers Delight," I immediately flipped the record over. It had an instrumental and I attempted to do my rhymes over it. But none of my rhymes would fit a beat. They wouldn't flow properly.

Still, that's how I got the rap bug. I thought I already knew how to rap back in '76. Now I had to rethink it a bit, had to tailor my writing and storytelling to come in over a beat. And I developed my own distinctive style. I'd taken my name as a tribute to Iceberg, and then it hit me one day—dude is a *writer.* I thought he was fly because he was a pimp, but I realized that I really admired him because he was a *writer.* There were a thousand pimps on the street but I liked Iceberg because he was able to articulate the life. And I started to develop those same skills in my rhymes, painting these dark portraits of the world of pimps, hustlers, and gangbangers.

On my second album *Power,* I laid it down:

I'm livin large as possible
Posse's unstoppable
My style is topical

Vividly optical

Listen and you'll see 'em

Sometimes I'll be 'em

That became the signature Ice-T style—rhymes that were "topical" and "vividly optical." To me it was street-level journalism, real-life observations told in poetry. That's the vision I tried to bring to all my recordings.

Now, I was going to parties around town with my DJ equipment. But I found that I was getting way more attention picking up the mic and rapping than I was from carrying them damn speakers! So what happened was, instead of busting my ass to throw my own parties, I started to go around from party to party, just to pick up the mic and rap.

My style was still really raw. But since everybody else was *terrible,* I was considered all right. That's when I first dipped my feet into the rap scene and hooked up with Evil E. and Henry G. Those cats were from New York, and they were called the New York City Spin Masters. We first met at a rap contest, and we immediately vibed. The New York City Spin Masters were already throwing these big parties. I went along with them on the party circuit, and while they would DJ, I'd get on the mic and spit. That's how I got my rap name going.

But while this was going on at nighttime, simultaneously, in the daytime—fuck it, I needed to get paid. Rap wasn't paying me shit. So that's when I got into the criminal game fulltime. And that's how I nearly got my ass killed.

I'D DONE MY SHARE of petty crime in high school—boosting car stereos, selling dime bags of weed and bullshit—but it wasn't until those first months back from the Army that my life of crime kicked into high gear.

It was easier for me to get into the life because Adrienne and I had broken up. Times had changed; we'd both changed. Adrienne was my first relationship, but we weren't under any illusions; we both knew I wasn't her life-long partner. We were together because of a pregnancy, and when I came home with my honorable discharge, we separated.

By the time my hustling life commenced in earnest, Adrienne had already started dating other people, and we weren't living together. I liked it that way, because hustling is a lifestyle best undertaken solo. Of course, I had to take care of my daughter, and no matter what, I would always support her. Hustling is a twenty-four-hour-a-day job. There are no vacations or downtime. Things were constantly crazy and hectic. For me, this was a serious transition from the regimented, structured time in the Army. I was essentially homeless, bouncing from place to place, living in the streets. I didn't want to bring that hustling world, with the constant risk and danger, around my baby daughter.

I was now running with some serious criminals. Understand: We were all hustlers from Crip neighborhoods—cats from the Rollin' 30s Original Harlem Crips—but we weren't about the gangbanging. We were *hustlers.*

Gangbanging and hustling are polar opposites. Gangbangers are about territory, power, and instilling fear in their enemies. Hustlers are about making money, twenty-four-hour scheming, always trying to get paid. From the minute we woke up, we were constantly scheming to rob someplace. Pulling licks. We'd stand around, playfully taunting each other. "What? You scared of money? Nigga, you scared of money?"

That one phrase sent more people to prison in my neighborhood than anything else.

I was hitting the street with four years of training as an elite soldier. I also had four years of pent-up energy and frustration. Life at Schofield Barracks had been so tightly regimented: up before dawn, constantly marching in formation, spit-shining boots, out on the firing range, getting my ass chewed out by the sergeant. I never regretted my four years in the Army. It definitely gave my life some discipline and structure. But after four years, I was ready to break out of that fucking mold.

There's something civilians often don't realize about the military. You're really only trained to do two things: Kill people and take over shit. You're not coming home with too many other useful skills, unless you plan on becoming a police officer. Today, we've got young vets touching down from Iraq and Afghanistan who've killed a shitload of people, and if they're not properly reprogrammed to come back into society, it's not like that "kill switch" is an easy thing to turn off. . . .

I quickly found that the operational theory hardwired into me from the years of Army life could be put to use on the streets. I got a reputation as the guy who could lay out a criminal operation with precision. Some of the licks we pulled are legendary, still talked about in the Cali streets. I always tell people there's no reason to lie about my past: The truth is *much* more insane.

THERE WERE HUSTLERS who liked to pull licks on the spur of the moment, but for me the art of the hustle was putting days—sometimes weeks—into the tactics and strategy. Most hustlers in South Central never strayed far from the block. Or the furthest they'd go to rob was the Crenshaw Shopping Center. Their reasoning was, the closer they stayed to home the less likely the cops would be to find them.

That wasn't my crew's style. We wanted to rob as far away from our 'hood as possible. If we robbed anywhere near L.A., we'd pick a spot in, say, Pacific Palisades, a twelve-mile drive on the freeway from Crenshaw Boulevard. But I was very choosy about the licks I'd organize. Sometimes a cat would come in and say, "Yo, I found a spot on Wilshire."

"You crazy?" I'd say. "Right in the *middle* of Beverly Hills! A nigga can't even *jog* down the street there without attracting the police."

For sure, Beverly Hills was a prime target. The whole area reeks of money, but my crew would never touch it. One day, these cats did try to take off the Beverly Wilshire Hotel. That was a hardcore crew from another neighborhood. They went in there with a mess of guns, and that shit got hectic. Real ugly.

See, nobody smart fucked with Beverly Hills. You could try to rob some ritzy hotel or caked-out jewelry store, but you'd never get out of there.

People from the crew were always looking for a perfect lick so we had a semi-permanent system of out-of-town scouting. We always tried to deliberate long and hard. We were serious criminals at this point. We'd wake up in the morning, thinking, *Where's the next lick?* It's twisted, I know, but this was our career choice.

Once we committed to that life, it was *on*. For about a year, motherfuckers wreaked havoc, first in Cali, then all the way across the United

States. We went out to Salt Lake City. We went out to Arizona. We hit jewelry stores and boutiques all up and down the Pacific Northwest Coast. We saw that, security-wise, the rest of the country wasn't as tight as L.A. We crisscrossed the whole country pulling licks, went all the way east. Some cats even left the United States for Europe and the Caribbean. We had our own little international crime spree. One of my partners got captured a few years later, and the cops fingerprinted him and ran him through the system. He had fifty-two aliases. Fifty-two fucking aliases! He gave a different name during each arrest.

He's in prison today doing twenty-five years.

5.

I WASN'T PLANNING ON getting locked up for a *week,* let alone hearing some judge handing me down a prison sentence with football numbers. As I mentioned, I'd spend days—sometimes weeks—planning a lick. We'd have to case the store, do our surveillance and recon. If it was a high-end spot, a few days before the lick I'd go in there with a girl hustler from our clique. We'd dress up in tennis outfits, K-Swiss and Polo, flashing Rolexes on our wrists. Of course, when you case a spot, you want to look like you've already *got* money. We'd pretend to be browsing, talking to the salesgirl, "Yes, miss, I was thinking of getting this piece as an anniversary gift for my great-aunt." All the time, we're taking mental notes, sizing up the alarm system, the layout of the store, the vulnerable points of entry, the make and model of the safe.

That's one thing I'll give to my four years in the Army. The military had given me that sense of articulating the mission and knowing how to delegate tasks: who was going to be the wheel man, who was going to be lookout, who was going to be the "basher"—the cat responsible for making the actual entry.

Without giving up too much game, the real trick to any crime is figuring out where you're going *after* you do it. In other words, if you're going to target a store in a big mall, you don't just do the lick and run. That's a guaranteed ticket to jail. No, you start where you want to end up, two blocks over, and you walk that path backward. That way, your escape route is your route to the lick. So if we're going to go in the mall, we're going to park two floors down on a motorcycle. Then we're going to figure out how we're going to go through the catacombs of the building and come up the back entrance. We'll pop out that entrance into the mall, and look for a target very close to that exit. The minute we hit it, we'll take about five steps and be out of that main area of the mall. We'll be back in the catacombs, going through doorways with security at our backs. But wherever there are locked doors, we've taken the extra step to duct tape the locks backward, so when we're leaving, we can prevent security from chasing us.

The getaway is actually more important than anything that happens during the robbery itself. If you practice your getaway, if you visualize yourself in the role of the person in hot pursuit of you, you're making sure that they can't follow this maze that you've created.

I took my time and planned so carefully for one simple reason: I did not want to get caught!

Now, when I got into the game, it was the dawn of the "bash" robbery. In fact, I think I went on perhaps the first recorded bash, which took place in a mall in Carson. It might have been done someplace else before us, but I know my crew had a lot to do with spreading the craziness across the country. The stores weren't ready for the bash. This was pre-Plexiglas. Most jewelry stores didn't have armed guards. They weren't ready for a bold, blatant robbery crew whose only tools were brains, balls, and an easily concealable baby sledgehammer.

The beauty of the basic bash was that there were no guns involved and it was lightning-quick. Three of us would walk into the jewelry store. One of us would take off a nice gold chain and tell the one lady working, "Would you please clean this chain?"

She goes to the back, and before she knows it we've whipped out the baby sledge, broken the display glass, grabbed a couple of trays of Rolexes, and bounced.

I laid it all out in my record, "That's How I'm Livin'":

> **Baby sledgehammers were the tools**
> **I speak on this with hesitation**
> **Even though we're passed the statute of limitations**

Yeah, baby sledgehammers were our tools. We were like hawks and those trays of high-end Rolexes were our prey. Rolexes were selling for $2,500 a piece on the street, and you could move them quick. So Swiss watches were cake. If you could take ten Rolexes during a bash, you could clear $25,000 in one day. That's another thing about robbery as your vocation: Just as essential as mapping out your escape routes is having established, safe networks to move the goods. If you sell that shit out of your trunk, you'll get caught. No question. See, everything in the game is highly specialized. Very rarely do you run across a successful all-around criminal. There's cats who specialize in robbery. There's cats who specialize in fencing. In the 'hood, there's networks of drug dealers and ballers who'll buy the stolen merchandise wholesale—doesn't matter what it is: jewelry, fur coats, designer clothes—and then they'll resell it on the street at a nice profit.

Some of the crews got more messy and more reckless with it.

We used to have a code. Right before I pulled the hammer out, I'd say "Is it a bet?"

I've got the baby sledgehammer stuck in the back of my waistband. I'm getting ready to grab the head of the hammer and come out with it. When that hits the glass, that shattering sound scares the shit out of people.

And if my partner says, "Naw, it's not a bet," I'd keep the baby sledge in my waistband. If he says, "It's a good bet"—SMASH!

Two sets of eyes were needed for confirmation. Almost like requiring two keys to arm a bomb. If my partner sees something's off, we're pulling out.

BACK AT THE CRIB, I was getting even more meticulous. I'd lay out maps of the city, circling the location of the lick in red pen, marking the nearest police stations, the various getaway routes, and the quickest access to freeways. We always worked on the five-minute rule. We figured we'd have five minutes to get in and out after we tripped the security system and before the cops arrived. Didn't matter if the alarms were sounding, we'd stay focused, never panicking, because we knew the cops couldn't respond before we'd clean out the store and be gone.

We loved to hit those mall jewelry stores, but nothing easy lasts forever, and the stores started to get wise to the bash. They upped their security systems. They started to lock the best pieces in safes, and that meant you couldn't get to them without holding the store employees at gunpoint.

No problem; there were plenty of other targets. After a while, I realized we could make just as much money, taking much less risk, if we targeted leather boutiques. One night we left one spot *empty*—took every single leather coat, jump suit, and handbag in the store. The best licks were stores that carried Gucci and Louis Vuitton bags, because we found we could sell those for $1,000 or $1,200 per bag. A good night's work stealing Gucci and Louis was just as big a score as pulling a big jewelry heist.

Man, we pulled some incredible licks. One time we went into a department store and cleared out *literally* all their minks. They had a mink case, with about twenty-five minks, and it was right by an exit. We waited, we pretended to browse, we went into the mink area. The case was open. There was one lady working there. We just looked at her. What is she gonna do? It ain't her shit, she doesn't have a gun. Is she really going risk her life for these fucking minks?

It just took nuts.

I reached in and grabbed a whole rack. My partner reached in and cleaned out the other rack. Cleaned 'em out.

We started heading toward the emergency exit. And since we'd done all our advance operational planning, we knew the layout. All department stores have catacombs—if you look at a diagram of a huge store like Macy's, Bloomingdale's, or May Company, you'll see that there's a whole world, invisible to the average person, on the sides and below the shopping spaces. We snatched all the furs and disappeared into the catacombs, moving too fast for any pursuit.

We got outside and were laughing because we'd got away so easily. As I looked at the mountain of mink and fox coats, I was already doing the mental calculations and figured they were worth maybe $50,000. We could sell them that same night for about $10,000. We started loading and stuffing all the minks into the trunk, backseat, and front seat and got into our car. We couldn't see out the windows because the mink was piled all the way up. The driver had to clear a little rectangular space so he could see where he was going. When we pulled away in the car, people kept staring at us and laughing, because we looked like a fucking furball driving down the street.

BUT NO MATTER HOW CAREFULLY you lay out your operational plans, just like in actual combat, there's always some unpredictable shit that can fuck up the mission. This one hot September night—Santa Ana winds blowing dry desert air through the city—we were pulling a lick at a mall on Western, going up toward Pico, as you start to get toward the Koreatown area. This wasn't a big-money lick, wasn't a jewelry store with hundreds of thousands in diamonds on display. For more than a week, we'd cased this Asian boutique specializing in designer bags and imported perfume located in a strip mall. The store almost looked like an airport duty-free shop. Nothing but the high-end shit. The good thing about robbing a mall: Nobody has guns. It's a safe lick. If somebody's going to chase you, odds are it's a Good Samaritan, or it's going to be people on walkie-talkies.

Rule one of any lick: You never rob in your own car. Some cats are stupid enough to steal cars in their neighborhood, but that's the very place the cops are going to start their search. We'd head out to the Valley, down to Long Beach, or out by LAX to steal a "G." We always picked older cars, Fords, Pontiacs, Chevrolets. In those days, pre–electronic ignition, a snatch bar wasn't needed; a car could be stolen in twenty seconds with a pair of pliers or a screwdriver. Didn't really matter what kind of car we stole, because after the lick, we were going to ditch the G anyway.

There were four of us that night: Nat the Cat's brother, Bebop, me, and two chicks. We showed up at that strip mall in an old rusted-out Pontiac we'd boosted. All the stores were deserted, all the lights were dark, even the supermarket down the block. There were no burglar bars on this Asian boutique, and we bashed through the lock in no time.

The alarm sounded, piercing the 2 AM silence, but we sparked the flashlights and got right down work. No one was talking, just snatching up the Gucci and Louis bags under the glare of our flashlights. The burglar alarm was screeching, but we'd done this drill so many times, we kept our focus. Just stay cool and steal as much shit as you can carry.

It was a running joke within our crew: Whenever we pulled a lick, I always wanted to stay in longer than anyone else. It took me years to analyze why. I finally realized that I wanted to stay in longer than anyone else because I fucking *hated* stealing. In fact—this may sound funny—I hated stealing so much that I did it with a *passion*. I felt, once I'm doing it, I got to do it well. If I'm robbing you, then you're gonna get fucking robbed, 'cause I hate the fact that I'm robbing you. I'm not just taking a little; I'm taking everything you got. I'm cleaning you the fuck out.

I'm in there, and there's this chick named Tanya next to me grabbing up designer handbags by the armful. The alarm has been going off for about four minutes, so we know it's nearly time for us to break.

Suddenly, I look back and Tanya has this terrified look in her eyes. Without a word, she makes a dash out the front door.

I turn and see a security guard in a black uniform running hard toward us. And then I see that the dude is armed. *Where'd this muthafucka come from? He damn sure ain't no cop.*

The guy had been on night watch at the supermarket down at the end of the mall. I was so deep in the store, so in my mental zone, everyone else had broken out. After Tanya, I was the last one running out the store with my arms full of designer bags.

The security guard was about twenty feet away with a pistol. He centered that shit on me. He shouted, "Freeze!"

I said to myself, *Naw—this fool ain't gonna shoot.*

I dropped the leather bags, ducked, ran off to the right.

He blasted at me. Took out a window right over my head.

Plate glass shattered, showering my neck and shoulders. My sneakers were crunching glass, and the cement was shimmering like someone had split open a piñata filled with diamonds.

I was running low, in a half-crouch, and he kept busting shots, taking out more and more windows. No hesitation—some real cowboy shit. The guy blasted out every goddamn window of that mall aiming for my head.

I bolted around the corner, and my crew was in the old Pontiac, moving toward me, but on some slow-roll shit. They wheeled up so close to the mall that the shattered windows were showering the car. I positioned myself to dive headfirst through the back window. But as I dove, the molding from the inside of the car door shot through my pant leg. I was stuck with my body half in the car, my leg sticking out the back window, and this fucking maniac Wyatt Earp security guard getting ready to take another shot at me.

I looked up at Bebop behind the wheel.

"Drive, muthafucka, drive!"

He gunned the G out of the parking lot, ran a red light, and we were on the freeway in minutes. Somehow, I managed to pull my body into the car and took a few deep breaths. The hot desert wind was replaced by the smell of new leather; the G was packed with all the Gucci and Louis bags we'd managed to carry. No one said shit until we were halfway back to South Central. Then we all busted out a crazy laugh.

To this day, I don't know how I escaped with my skull intact. When I got back to the crib, my girl was half-asleep in bed. She kissed me, stroking my neck, and suddenly let out a little gasp.

"What's the matter, baby?" she said.

She pulled away from me, turned on the bedroom lights. There was a drop of blood on her fingertip.

We went into the bathroom, and she must have spent thirty minutes picking out all those tiny pieces of glass from my hair.

———

THE GAME WAS SO DIFFERENT in my day. You didn't have DNA testing to worry about if you got cut reaching into the glass case during a
bash. Nobody was even thinking about hidden cameras or videotape.

Funny thing is, some spots *did* have security cameras, and apparently
I did get captured on videotape. Years after I got out of the robbery
game, when I was already steadily working as an actor, one of my former crime partners went to a funeral and the police picked him up.
They'd had him under surveillance and grabbed him up on an out-
standing warrant. He had two different IDs on him. He's an ex-con, so
they were busting his balls. In the midst of questioning—for some
fucking reason—he blurted out: "No officers, I'm in the entertainment
business. I work with Ice-T."

One of the cops said, "Fuck Ice-T. Ice-T hangs with a den of thieves.
You tell Ice-T to keep his nose clean. We got enough film on him to
make a fuckin' movie."

By that time, I was already out of the robbery life. The statute of limitations had long passed on any of my crimes.

And when my buddy called me to tell me this, I screamed on him.

"Nigga, what the fuck? I don't do shit anymore! I'm *square*. Didn't
they get the memo?"

THESE DAYS PEOPLE CONSTANTLY ASK ME how I could go from
being a stone criminal to playing a cop for ten years on *Law & Order*.
Some cats try to make it like I'm a hypocrite, or two-faced, or some
bullshit.

Listen, when you're in the life of crime, it's true, you feel like you're
in a fraternity. There are people out there that really *love* to break the
law; they're antisocial, always in that fucking zone. But I never was that
kind of cat. I didn't *hate* the police. As a matter of fact, I think if you're
a real crook, you better have *respect* for the cops. Otherwise you're going
to get caught.

But don't get it twisted. I never had any allegiance to crime. I just
wanted the paper. I lived that life because there was a time when I
thought I could do it, an era when every day I thought I was smarter
than the police. I took pride in outsmarting them.

I used to always tell Sean E. Sean and my boys, "The cops' job is to watch the line. My job is to step over and back." I took pride in the fact that I could step over and back without getting caught. Criminals think they're slick. It's the ego pump you get, like John Dillinger, smirking, "They have to watch every bank. I only have to pick *one.*" There's nothing more dangerous than a successful criminal. He's got so much attitude. And, hell yeah, I've been that monster.

WHILE OUT THERE HUSTLING, hitting jewelry licks, I was getting into Iceberg Slim books—really deep. Memorizing every word Iceberg wrote. Through those books and my time in Hawaii around Mac and the other pimps, I'd soaked up the game. It seemed so intriguing, honestly, that I just wanted to try my hand at it.

Let me preface this by saying one thing: Pimpin' is not by any means an *honorable* hustle. It's just like stealing cars, robbing banks, or selling drugs. It's *negative.* People romanticize bank robbers like Dillinger and Jesse James. People romanticize jewel thieves. People romanticize mobsters like Al Capone and John Gotti. There's a similar mystique to the pimp.

But there is nothing positive about pimpin'. It's just like any other criminal game. And most people who talk about pimpin' don't even know what they're talking about.

When someone comes up to me today and says, "Yo, Ice, I'm pimpin'," usually he's not. Usually he's just a *player,* a guy who's got a lot of girls. But it's fashionable these days to call yourself a pimp. Pimpin' is a lot more than having a nice lifestyle, a sexy car, and a gang of girls around you all the time.

During the height of our robbery sprees, we had to go on the lam. The situation in L.A. was too hot for a minute. Everyone in our organization had to go out of town until shit cooled down. I went back to Hawaii, and I connected with the same folks out there, Mac and the other pimps. Mac was steadily pushing that ism: "Yo, Ice, you need to be *doing* this. This is something you're cut for."

I thought about it while I was in Hawaii. When I came back to L.A., it wasn't nothin' to put a couple of girls in motion. But as the famous saying goes: Pimpin' ain't easy. No, as a matter of fact, it's very fucking complicated. It's the type of game where you'll end up pulling your hair out before you learn to do it correctly. That's why I never claim I was some stand-up pimp, doing it full-time, sending girls out there on the track for years and years. There are so many levels of the game. The most basic is just "sending a bitch." Most guys—even entry-level pimps—have "sent a bitch." Yeah, I've done it. And I still know how to do it. Even if I'm not pimpin' today, I know the fundamentals.

It's been said that trying to teach pimpin' to a square is like trying to teach astrophysics to a wino. But that question comes to me a lot: What's pimpin'?—so I'll break it down simply. Basically you're turning the game that the girls use on men back on themselves. You're flipping it completely. When a typical guy meets a hot girl, he'll say, "Man, I'll do *anything* for her. I'll give her all my money. I'll buy her anything if she'd just give me some play." That's the guy's mentality.

The pimp is the reverse of that. He spins that mental one hundred eighty degrees on the woman. The pimp thinks, "If I'm marrying you, then why the fuck am *I* on my knees?" The first agenda of the pimp is to be hotter, flyer, better-looking than the girl. That's the reason pimps wear expensive tailor-made suits, why they wear gators, why their hair grows longer than the girls. Their job is to outmatch the female in everything. Rule one: You have to be finer than the girl. You do that so that she feels like she's stepping up in the world by being with you.

There's another common expression in the pimp game: "Every man cannot accept ho money." If a guy meets a stripper and likes her— maybe his dumb ass even falls in love—the man's natural instinct is to tell her to stop stripping. He's a square dude so he wants to turn her into a square chick. Happily ever after, two kids and a dog on a quiet block in the suburbs. All that Hallmark-card bullshit. But the pimp, he doesn't try to "reform" her; he feeds into the negativity that she's already living. If a girl's working as a stripper, she can't have a girl for a roommate who's trying to scold her, make her feel guilty, saying: "Why do you do that? Why do you strip? You're demeaning yourself!" No, she needs a roommate that backs her agenda: "Ooh, girl, I like them shoes! We gonna *break* them dudes tonight!"

Rather than a girlfriend, the pimp is a male that reinforces the negativity.

Real pimps do not pimp square girls. That's a huge misconception. There's a fear out there in the square world that a pimp is going to find some nice middle-American girl—an apple-cheeked cheerleader from the suburbs—and turn her into a prostitute. That's not going to happen. The only pimps that do that are known as "gorilla pimps," and they're not even respected in the game. They're basically kidnappers and sex traffickers. They're seen as scumbags. No one considers them real pimps. A gorilla pimp will snatch up a girl, get her high, lock her up someplace, then rape her and make her have sex for money—but the girl is going to run as soon as she sees a chance to escape. That's not a pimp. Real pimps say, "It's by choice, not by force."

Choosing is the key word in the pimp game. Because you can't convince a girl to give you her money. No amount of sweet-talking in the world is going to do that. She has to want to. She has to choose to do that.

That's why pimps dress so outrageously. It's full-disclosure. Like truth in advertising. When you get into real heavy pimpin', you'll see the most outlandish fashion statements. "Yo, I got on a canary-yellow suit, bitch. *Come on!* You know what this is." That yellow suit is like a billboard saying, "I'm not trying to attract a square broad. I'm trying to attract a broad that knows what this game is and wants to be part of it."

Pimps don't hide behind the bushes, pretending to be some UPS man. They're flamboyant as fuck. They're peacocks of the street. And trust me—there are hundreds and hundreds of girls who are attracted to that game.

What pimps live by day-to-day is the act of sending the woman to go get money from a trick. The thing of it is, even without pimps, girls do it to guys all the time. When a woman goes on a date with a man that she doesn't like—just for the dinner, or a pair of shoes, or some jewelry—that's a form of hoin'. Anytime a girl does anything sexually to get something material in return without really caring about the guy—don't kid yourself—that's hoin'.

The pimp takes that same energy and harnesses it. After the girl works the trick out of his money, the pimp relieves the girl of her money. Not by threatening her. He gets the money by creating an illusion in her mind that he's some kind of boyfriend. "Baby," he tells her, "give me the money—I'll give you what you need, whatever you want—but I'll manage this dough better than you."

What the pimp says to the girl is, "Hey, if you really like me, you'll give me your money. You won't give me sex; you give sex to the tricks. To prove you love me, you'll give me paper." Also, almost all pimps have some big creative master plan. They act like streetwise geniuses. Carry themselves like the masters of the universe. "Yo baby," they say, "we're going to make this big money. We're going to do big things." The girls buy into this mega-plan—even if it's all a delusion—and that's what bonds them to the pimp, the notion they're going to elevate themselves by staying with him.

Pimpin' isn't necessarily sending a girl to the track. It's sending the girl anywhere to get money from a trick and bring it back to you. Doesn't even need to be full-blown sex, as long as she's using her feminine ways to get that paper. Take a stripper. We call stripping "the indoor track." A stripper in a decent club can make $500 a night. So an average stripper will go out the first two nights, make enough money for the week and then she won't work. She'll chill until she needs more money. But not when she's got a pimp. A pimp's got three feet: Two on the ground, and one in your ass. He motivates the girl to get out there the other five days of the week, too, just to maximize the hustle.

Like I said, pimpin' is a very *negative* aspect of our society. But I think my man Kenny Ivey put it best in an episode of *Pimps Up, Ho's Down.* "If there wasn't no pimps," Kenny said, "there'd still be a *hell* of a lot of hoin' going on."

THE GAME IS AN ENTIRE BOOK unto itself. But this is probably the best window I can give you into the pimpin' dynamic.

If you could be invisible, sitting inside a car with four women on the way to some club, what would be the conversation?

"Oh, I hope I see homeboy with his girl. I'm'a tell!"

"I'm gonna go get pregnant by this dude."

"He's gonna take me shopping this weekend."

"Girl, I hope I meet a millionaire."

Not a *nice*-looking guy. Not a *decent,* hardworking dude. No, I hope I meet a goddamn *millionaire.*

Now let's take four guys on the way to the same club. What are the guys talking about?

"I wanna fuck."

"I wanna fuck."

"I wanna fuck."

"Man, if you fuck, can I fuck?"

It's one-dimensional. Simple and obvious. And it's harmless—truthfully. Guys on the way to a club sound like cartoons, like Yogi Bear and Boo Boo talking about getting laid.

The girls' car is far more diabolical and cunning. Sex is set up as if it's the big determining factor in the male–female dynamic. But to me—from the pimp point of view—it's not sex. It's *always* money.

Now—you make the guys' car have the girls' conversation, *then* you have a car full of pimps.

6.

IN HUSTLING WE ALWAYS SAY, "You raise the risk, you raise the prof-
its."

Of course, the bashes were bound to escalate. Cats wanted to stay in
the store longer; they wanted to steal more and more. Greed is such a
primal human characteristic. Give a dude a chance to clear $10,000 a
day, he's going to start saying, "Why can't I make $20,000? Why can't
I take $40,000?"

So as the bashes became more dangerous, more violent, a lot of my
friends went under—because they got a little too aggressive. Violence is
always going to bring heat from the cops.

Even as deep as I was in that life of crime, I never wanted to hurt anybody. And despite the military training—or, who knows, maybe because of it—I was never into using firearms during a robbery. I always
felt if I pulled a gun during a crime that gave somebody the right to
shoot me dead.

The licks escalated to another level; they morphed into what were
called "pistol bashes." A pistol bash is an armed robbery, plain and sim-

ple. You still smash the display glass with the sledgehammer, but one of your crew simultaneously holds everyone in the store at gunpoint. That to me was just too high-risk. What if some innocent bystander panics? What if someone decides to play Good Samaritan? What if an off-duty cop is shopping for a tennis bracelet for his anniversary? It just wasn't worth it to me to go on any pistol bashes.

I got challenged a lot by my boys for backing away from those gun jobs.

"Ice, you scared."

"Yeah, nigga, you scared of money."

And I'd say, "Naw, I'm just not with that."

All criminals have certain things they don't want to do; you've got to follow your gut in the game. You don't ignore your gut instinct. Otherwise, that's when you end up in jail sitting, muttering, "Shit, I knew I shouldn'ta . . ."

I didn't leave the game overnight. But I refused to go on any of the pistol bashes, and most of the cats I really respected got cracked. One by one, I watched them all get locked up. Eventually I started working with second-string players. It wasn't the same caliber crook.

I remember this one day: straight baby sledgehammer jewelry lick. I had this cat I didn't know too well named Jimmy working it with me. We got out of the mall with all the Rolexes we could carry. But we had a pretty complicated escape route to the getaway car. And we were sprinting, twisting, and turning. Every time we'd hit a corner, Jimmy would fall on his fucking ass. I paused and glanced down. This fool had on some fresh Gucci loafers. He was too stupid to wear sneakers like the rest of us.

"Stupid muthafucka!" I said, and then I kept running, whipping around corners. Our escape route really required some athleticism, ducking and hopping and going through all kinds of trick shit.

By the time we got to the car, this clown Jimmy was way behind us—couldn't see him anywhere. We got in the car and I was steaming because we should have been long gone, but we were still waiting for asshole in his Gucci loafers. Finally, I got out of the car looking for this dude. I saw Jimmy still trying to climb up this ivy-covered hill. I'd just run up the hill in my Adidas Shell Toes, but his dumb ass was stuck scrambling on the side, and I had to go back and get him. I grabbed his arm and helped him make it up the hill.

At the end of that lick we didn't want to pay him his cut. Jimmy started complaining but I told him to shut the fuck up.

"You fell a thousand times, nigga. Why'd we even *bring* you? Useless fuck. Plus you didn't have shit when you finally got to the car."

There's a basic rule to the robbery game: If you don't bring anything back to the getaway car—shit, you ain't getting nothing.

I WAS STUCK TRYING TO DO licks with second-string clowns like Jimmy, and at the same time, at night, I was still going out into the clubs and rapping. Hip-hop wasn't paying me, but it was an entertaining sideline to my criminal life. It's like I had a split-screen on my daytime and nighttime exploits. And in the lyrics, I was talking all about the game—but always in a certain, very deliberate way. I'd been warned by other hustlers, the boys in my crew.

"Yo, yo, Ice, don't say *too* much."

Today they got a term for it. Dry snitching. My boys put it this way: It would be a *real* bad move to put yourself or one of your boys in jail because of this rap bullshit.

"Don't worry," I told them. "I know how to do this." That was a skill in itself, being able to rap about the reality of crime without getting too specific.

Mostly, I was rapping live in the club, but this one day, I was sitting in Good Fred Beauty Salon on 54th and Western. Good Fred's was where I always went to get my hair done. As I waited for them to finish my perm, I started spitting some off-the-dome rhymes to the girls in the shop. I don't even remember what I was spitting: *I'm the hula dula, the whorehouse ruler. . . .* Back then I was only rapping about fly clothes, jewelry, and rides. It was confident player shit, because we were living it!

Out of the blue, this guy overheard me rhyming and stepped to me.

"Yo, player. You sound tight. You want to make a record?"

I thought the dude was trying to clown me. "Who the fuck are you?"

He told me his name was Willy Strong from Saturn Records. "We got our own recording studio," he said. "We could get you in the studio right now."

I didn't know if he was running a game on me or not, but what the hell? We went straight into the studio and we made my first record, "Cold Wind Madness"—also known as "The Coldest Rap." Willie Strong was the producer. He had a beat by Jimmy Jam and Terry Lewis. There were girls singing on one track—they erased the singing and I laid down my own vocal. Making the record was cool, but it was a novelty to me. I really didn't think I could make a dime rapping. Willie Strong pressed up the vinyl. Saturn had its own retail store called VIP Records on Crenshaw Boulevard and they started selling the shit out of "Cold Wind Madness."

But what happened next was kind of crazy. Alex Jordanoff and his boy K.K. owned a club in MacArthur Park called The Radio, which became a hugely influential nightspot in L.A. Alex and K.K. heard my record and started playing it in their club. I didn't know anything about it. I'd never even heard of The Radio. But my record was becoming real popular in the spot. Eventually, Alex and K.K. hunted me down through the VIP Records retail store and asked me if I'd come do a live performance.

So I showed up at The Radio, expecting nothing. Went in there to do my first performance of the record and I was bugged out. I'll never forget the scene: I got up to take the microphone, looking out at about three hundred people—almost all white, trendy kids—and from the opening lines, I saw everybody in this club nodding, waving their arms. They not only knew my song, they knew it word-for-fucking-word. And they were rapping it in perfect sync, too:

I'm a playa, that's all I know
On a summer day I play in the snow
From the womb to the tomb I run my game
'Cause I'm cold as Ice and I show no shame
The ladies say that I'm heaven-sent
'Cause I got more money than the U.S. Mint. . . .

"The Coldest Rap" hadn't been on any radio—most of the lyrics were way too hardcore for that. Certain clubs have a playlist, with the DJs spinning the same records every night, and they'd been playing my song every night in The Radio. After a few months of that heavy rotation, all The Radio regulars had it memorized.

That was another turning point in my life, seeing all these total strangers with their hands in the air, singing word for word what I'd written. Up to this moment, I'd never taken rapping seriously. I was too into hustling, too into having money. I was mad cynical and arrogant. I already had all the expensive jewelry and clothes I could wear. I already had a brand-new Porsche—I'd bitten the criminal apple, and when you bite that apple, you think everybody who works for a living is a sucker. You think they're all squares and you're flyer, you're slicker. Your ego just goes through the fucking roof. You're just a monster.

But that night in The Radio stripped away my hustler's attitude for a night. It brought me back to being a little kid. Like when you're dividing up teams for pickup football and one of your friends picks you first. *Man, the coolest kid thinks I can play!* It was a kind of validation— this more innocent validation—that was so foreign to the hustler's life.

After that little taste of success, I started to go back to the spot every weekend and perform. I had that swagger already; I had a performer's "presence." Alex Jordanoff put me in charge of the stage. I was their MC, the house rapper, and I selected who could come up onstage. And it was perfect timing; The Radio was becoming the club to be seen at. One night, Madonna came and performed. Adam Ant. Malcolm McLaren—rest in peace—came through a few times. The Radio was on the cutting edge of a new underground phenomenon, mixing hip-hop with a punk sensibility. All these white punks and new wave cats were trying to link up with hip-hop's edgier vibe, our rapping, our break-dancing, our street fashion.

When I became a fixture at The Radio, the club clientele was virtually 100 percent white kids. But over the weeks, I started to bring some of my black hustler friends from the 'hood. That was a weird warp. We had all the jewelry, the fly shoes, the expensive rides parked out front. We had all the entrapments of stardom already.

And even among L.A. hustlers, my clique—you have to remember—

felt we were elite. We only stole top-line jewelry, we drank Dom Pérignon, wore Louis Vuitton long before any cats in the hood had even heard of it. We knew about brands like Gucci and Fendi and stores like Neiman Marcus. If you want to track the movement, look at the movie *Breakin'*—that was shot in The Radio—and when I did my cameo, I had on this black Neiman Marcus hat. Dudes asked me what the fuck I was wearing. What was I doing in some Neiman Marcus hat? That wasn't a hip-hop look. Kangol was the cap all the B-Boys rocked.

But our fashion sense came from doing the licks. We'd go rob these expensive designer stores, so we had to have the expensive designer clothes. Meanwhile, a lot of my crime partners who'd been locked up when the licks started getting more violent were calling my crib. Every morning, I'd get these collect calls from the correctional facilities. My boys were all telling me the same thing: to be careful; prison had been heating up, too.

"Steer clear of this penitentiary," they said. "This ain't no place for no player, Ice. You got niggas here tying blue rags around their heads every morning. Niggas banging hard in here. Niggas here don't even know Dom Pérignon. Don't come to the pen, player."

I'D LISTEN TO THE WARNINGS, but the reality didn't really hit home until Sean E. Sean went under. Sean E. Sean was the weed man in the crew. Sean E. had been the weed man since high school. Sean and my man Vic—later known as Beatmaster V from Body Count—had a place down in Inglewood right off Crenshaw Boulevard that became this full-blown crime house. They were slinging serious amounts of weed. Not nickel and dime bags, but dozens of pounds stacked up everywhere.

I never was too down with the drug game. As I said, I never did weed or coke or any kind of drugs, but for a really brief time I tried to sell coke. Big headache. Everybody that I gave a bag of coke to never brought me my money. I was handing out blow to all my friends. A couple ounces here and there. And then you need to enforce that shit. I was trying to flip a key, but everybody came up short, and I realized I couldn't do it. I couldn't hurt my friends. Because if niggas don't pay you in the drug game, you have no choice but to hurt them. There is no layaway plan. There is no other option. You have to go straight to violence. I barely recouped the money I'd spent, and I said, "Naw, fuck that." I wasn't cut out to be a drug dealer.

But Sean E. Sean had a tight weed game, and his place in Inglewood was the spot. They'd just gotten twenty-six pounds of weed on consignment. I wasn't fucking with the weed end of the operation, but I was out doing licks on the other side of town. We did this truck lick— a hijacking—where we boosted tons of Technics turntables and stereo equipment and a gang of Canon cameras. All brand-new shit, still boxed up. We unloaded it all at Sean's crib in Inglewood.

It was the perfect drop house for us to use until we could figure out how to unload the swag. We also had a hot car—a Spitfire—parked in Sean's garage. Sean was so busy with the weed-slinging, he didn't know anything about all this shit from the hijacking. The hijacking charge alone carries twenty-five years, and the boosted Spitfire in the garage— well, that's grand theft auto.

Somehow the LAPD was tipped off, and before long, the cops raided the place. Busted Sean E. Sean and Beatmaster V with hella weed, plus all that hijacked swag and the stolen Spitfire.

When Sean E. got cracked, he said "Fuck it," and he took the case. He just stared at the cops. "Yeah, man, whatever. The shit's in my house, give me whatever you gotta give me. Fuck it."

They had him dead-to-right for the weed, but Sean held water. The LAPD tried to sweat him hard but they couldn't pin any hijacking on him. How could they? He wasn't fronting. He honestly didn't know jack shit about no truck hijacking! I hadn't told him; it was safer to compartmentalize our various hustles that way. The Feds tried to pressure Sean to snitch on whoever pulled the hijacking but he wouldn't tell. They hit him with possession of stolen merchandise, but those charges were eventually dropped. So Sean and Vic just ended up doing two years on the drug case.

Sean E. Sean's my boy for life. He could have hemmed and hawed. He could have said, "I don't know . . . some other cats left some of their shit here." But no. He held his own.

I don't even know if you call it loyalty. It's the code we lived by. In fact, didn't make much difference that we'd been homeys since Palms

Junior High and Crenshaw; Sean never once considered telling. That's just how he's cut.

I would have done the same thing for him. If I'm sitting in a house full of your stolen shit and I get cracked I'm not going to tell. I'm not going to put the weight on the next dude.

I'll say this, without any hesitation: If Sean E. Sean hadn't taken the weight, there would be no Ice-T today. Nobody would have heard of me. There'd be no records, no movies, no TV shows—you wouldn't be reading this book. I'd just be another brother who fucked his life up, spent his best years—twenty-five of them—in the pen over some dumb shit.

7.

WHEN I WASN'T RAPPING in The Radio, I would hang with my hustler friends in another club called Carolina West on Century Boulevard. All the big-time pimps in L.A. used to hang out at Carolina West. It was one of the few after-hours spots around and the club was open from 9 PM to 9 AM. The right time to get there was real late, like three in the morning. So I'd leave The Radio after the crowd thinned, hop in my Porsche, and get to Carolina West right as the club was getting good.

One night I was there by myself, hanging out, talking to girls. By the time I left, it was morning. I was at the intersection of West Boulevard and Slauson, stopped at a red light in my Porsche 914. I was wiped. I started half-dozing at the light—feeling like if I could just close my eyes for a second, I'd be okay to drive home, I'd get my second-wind . . .

I have no memory of this, but apparently my foot slipped off the brake and my Porsche rolled into the intersection. *Boom,* I got fucking broadsided. The car flipped and rolled. I didn't have my seatbelt on, and I got knocked into my passenger seat. The impact broke the steering wheel clean off, demolished the driver's side—my little Matchbox 914 had folded right in half.

I should have died that morning. To all the bystanders, I *looked* like a dead man. One of the L.A. papers actually reported it as a fatality. The reporter on the scene figured no one could have survived a wreck like that. The car was crushed; I was slumped there in the passenger seat, bleeding profusely and looking lifeless.

I wasn't dead, though I was completely unconscious for over a day. I had no ID on me at the time of the wreck. When you're hustling, you never carry any kind of identification so you can always give the cops an alias, and I had a fat knot of cash in my pocket. The paramedics and the police had no clue who I was.

They took me to L.A. County Hospital and I was John Doe'd up in there for a long time.

County is not a good place to be laid up. I was stuck in a room with ten people. When I came to—well, really I was drifting in and out of consciousness—I heard people moaning and screaming; a dude across from me had a colostomy bag; at one point, someone died right there in the room with me.

When you're in County, you don't talk to doctors much, you just get moved around on gurneys. But some doctor in a white coat finally came around and I overheard him telling a nurse how lucky I was to have pulled through. I had a broken pelvis, broken ribs, and a fractured femur. Everything on my left side was smashed and broken.

I was lucky, the doctor said to the nurse, because I was so healthy. I'd just come out of the military; I was in top physical shape. The fact that I was a healthy, young specimen meant that the trauma couldn't take me out. Even when I was unconscious, my body was fighting back with all its strength. If I was weaker, or if I'd abused my body with drugs and booze, I might not have pulled through.

At this stage of my life, I was basically a transient hustler. After my Jersey years and then living with my aunt in View Park—essentially, I didn't have a home life. I didn't have a house with real family. And for most of the time since I'd gotten out of the Army, I'd kept small apartments, so I would be in one neighborhood from day to day. Living the life of a full-time criminal, you're never too stationary. You have to move around. Sean E. Sean lived in the same neighborhood in the hills where my aunt lived. But he'd already been locked up. And anyway, if I didn't see homeys like Sean E. Sean or Sean E. Mac for a week or two, it was no big deal. This was long before the era when dudes were checking in with each other every few hours on their cells or text messaging. You could have close homeys and not see them or hear from them for weeks, and it was no cause for alarm.

Therefore when I came up missing, it took a *long* time for folks to realize I was even gone. My daughter and my baby's mother didn't miss me. Nobody noticed I wasn't around. The people I saw regularly were the crew from the nightclubs: the white dudes I rapped for down at The Radio; the hustlers and ballers I used to hang with at Carolina West. Nightclub friends act like they're your family when you're out in the spot; but it's not like they gave a fuck when I didn't show up for a couple weeks.

I was in really bad shape. I needed constant cycles of pain medication for my injuries. I remember lying there, hooked on the pain pills. One afternoon the nurse didn't give me my pain pills—she made a mistake and skipped me during her rounds—and I had to wait four hours for the next dose. I tried to tell the nurse I needed my medication and she said, "No, you got them already." She thought I was lying. You know, like I was a junkie trying to con her for an extra dose.

I was arguing with her, but then it was like a switch went off. I could no longer even speak. The pain suddenly kicked in. I could feel *all* my broken bones. I was screaming, but the nurse still wouldn't give me the meds, and I knocked over the drinks on my table, my legs were kicking. I was just wilding out. All the nurses did was wheel me out into the middle of the floor so I couldn't kick over anything else.

I never saw combat during my military service, but I now realize how you could be seriously banged up and not realize how severe your injuries are until you come off those drugs. When the painkillers wear off, you feel every broken bone, every bruise, every cut, every single *piece* of pain. . . .

It was a hellish four hours. Excruciating. I actually thought I was dying. Then at the end of the four hours, the nurse came to find me still screaming and thrashing. Finally she gave me my pills. I gulped them down, and the meds hit me so hard, it felt like I dissolved through the mattress. I was melting into this euphoric, pain-free state. That's when I realized how many drugs I was on, because I couldn't feel the broken bones anymore.

So I ended up lying there as a John Doe in L.A. County for several weeks, until my buddy Sean E. Mac's mother realized I was missing. Somehow or other—I still don't know exactly—Sean E. Mac and his moms tracked me down. His moms told everyone at County that I'd been in the military, that I'd done four years of service with an honorable discharge, and just like that, they put me in an ambulance and transferred me to the Veterans Administration Hospital over in Westwood. Life got a lot better in the V.A. Hospital. I ended up getting my own private room.

Due to the nature of my injuries, they couldn't put casts on me, so I was in a light form of traction for ten straight weeks. Completely immobile. You sit there ten weeks, even if you got a few folks coming to see you, it's not like you've got a gang of family waiting there with balloons and bouquets for you to get discharged. I was pretty much isolated lying there in traction, in my quiet private room at the V.A. Hospital. Lying in the hospital, all plastered up like a mummy, hooked up to IVs and beeping monitors, I had nothing but time to reflect on that transient hustling life I was leading. Being banged up in the hospital—it's almost like being in jail—I realized who was really on my team. I realized what I actually had in my life—and what I was missing.

It felt like *no one* came to visit me, but the truth is I was so doped up on pain meds I didn't know what was going on around me. I remember one time that Sean E. Mac's sister came up to visit me, and I had a catheter up my dick and I just lay there talking to her, mumbling away, with my whole shit exposed. Later on, Sean E. Mac came up to my room. He said, "Ice, what's up? You were so fucked up you showed my sister your fucking balls!"

One day I had a preacher coming through asking me to pray with him. Wanting to know if I'd share the "Good Word" with him. It was the only time in my life when I even contemplated testing out religion to see if it fit me. Finally I told the preacher, "Naw, I'm not gonna pray, I just wanna make myself get better."

These religious cats were going around praying over people, and I told them I didn't want anyone praying over me. I remember shouting, "I ain't dying!" 'Cause to me that shit felt too much like giving the last rites when everything is hopeless.

Being immobile gave me a long time to lay there and think, to reflect on my situation. To finally see life on balancing scales. Not in the religious sense of those preachers talking about Judgment Day—though maybe that put the idea in my head. I started to weigh out all the things I wanted to accomplish and all the things I hadn't yet done. And then this crashing feeling hit me, this sense of, *Okay, motherfucker. That was your life. And really, be honest with yourself: You didn't do shit.*

I wasn't depressed. I truly felt I'd done nothing, absolutely nothing. And so I flashed back to that moment at Schofield Barracks when Sergeant Donovan screamed that I couldn't make it in the civilian world. And here I was nearly dead, and if I'd died in that Porsche, I'd have lived my whole life without accomplishing anything.

WHEN I CAME OUT of the hospital, I couldn't walk well. I was limping along, sometimes with a cane. I had a lot of trauma in my hip area, but old habits die hard, and for some insane reason I still thought I could pull licks. There was no way I could run, let alone climb or fight. And most of the licks we were doing were very physical. At some point you needed to do something athletic or acrobatic, whether it was sprinting away from the store, or jumping headfirst into a slow-rolling car. It was action-packed and you had to be in top physical condition.

I didn't want to use my cane, so I was hobbling around, real slow. It took me at least a month out of the hospital to be able to walk without a limp. I definitely wasn't able to run or fight anybody.

The thing about hustling, you have to weigh the odds: Sometimes you win, sometimes you lose. Sean was under. Tony was under. Vic was under. A lot of these cats that I looked up to were locked up. And I found myself hanging with second- and third-string players. Real scrubs. Dudes like Jimmy in the stupid-ass Gucci loafers.

I tried to get back in the game, working with these slapstick mother-fuckers. And then it dawned on me, *Ice, do you think you're that much smarter than all the guys that are stuck? They're under, they're behind the wall, telling you don't come to the pen. . . .*

You just have to change your hustle at some point. You have to tell yourself, "Yo, I can't do that wild shit no more."

Finally, a few weeks after being released from the V.A. Hospital, it clicked in my head. I said: *Let me stop running around with these hustlers— risking prison every single day. Let me give this rap game a shot.*

PART THREE

SIX IN THE MORNIN'

"IT AIN'T ABOUT THE COME-UP.

IT'S ABOUT THE COMEBACK."

—ICE-T'S DAILY GAME

8.

ONE SATURDAY NIGHT, about two weeks after being released from the V.A. Hospital, I went straight back to the Carolina West Club. There was an open mic competition and Kurtis Blow was the judge. But I didn't know that when I limped in there.

I grabbed the mic and I won first prize.

Just some kind of bullshit rhyming. I think I made up some raps at that point.

At that time, nobody had made any money rapping. It was just something to do for the hell of it.

When the crowd exploded and I won first place, I felt like that was a vote of confidence. Especially if a real rapper like Kurtis Blow from New York thought I could rap.

West Coast rap was kind of virgin territory. Besides the ones at The Radio, there were a few hip-hop parties popping up in L.A. like Uncle Jamm's Army. They had a DJ named Egyptian Lover and would throw big dances at the L.A. Sports Arena. For a long time, I was the only person they'd let rap at Uncle Jamm's Army. They had a drum machine and

Egyptian Lover or the other DJ, Bobcat, would shout, "We 'bout to go live" and then he'd play live beats and I'd rap over them.

After I made "The Coldest Rap," I recorded a couple tracks with this guy, David Storrs, who used to be a regular at The Radio. David Storrs was a white dude from Hollywood. He produced this track called "Reckless"—technically, the main performer was Chris "The Glove" Taylor, who was a DJ at The Radio. I was just a featured rapper on the track. But Dave Storrs could see I was the rising star. Then I made a couple of records with this cat named Unknown DJ.

Unknown had his own little label. He also had cats like King T and Compton's Most Wanted, and I was trying to get him to make a record with my DJ's brother, but he said, "Naw, Ice, why don't you do a record for me?" So I laid down "You Don't Quit," then I did "Dog'n the Wax," both of which had Unknown DJ's "electro-hop" production sound.

"Dog'n the Wax" needed a B-Side. So I wrote this rap called "6 in the Mornin'."

And that record just changed the whole game.

PEOPLE OFTEN SAY I created the gangsta rap genre with that record, but let me give proper credit. It was Schoolly D who inspired me to write the rhyme. I'd been in this club in Santa Monica, and I heard Schoolly D's "PSK" booming through the speakers. My jaw dropped. I turned to my homey and said, "Yo, this shit is so dusted!" It sounded different than regular hip-hop. It sounded like you were high, the way the beats were echoing, and his whole delivery was so crazy.

Schoolly D was writing about Park Side Killers, which is a Philly gang. But it was a very vague record. "PSK, we makin' that green, people always say what the hell does that mean?" Schoolly D says, "S for the way you scream and shout / One by one I'm knocking you out." That was the most violent thing he said in the whole record.

He was reppin' a set. He was repping PSK. But it wasn't too specific. He was just alluding to the gang life.

Now I took that inspiration and ran with it. I said, "Let's use that same dusted vibe, but let's tell an L.A. story with it."

I adopted a delivery similar to Schoolly D's but rapped about the shit

I knew firsthand. I wrote the lyrics in my apartment in Hollywood with
an 808 drum machine. The beat was kind of like a Beastie Boys record,
very minimal and raw; it was just meant to be something different—it
was a B-Side, so I was feeling loose and experimental. Nobody had ever
done a record with a scratch break: *bam-bam-bam*. It was so simple and
stripped down.

> **Six in the mornin' police at my door**
> **Fresh Adidas squeak across the bathroom floor**
> **Out the back window I make my escape**
> **Didn't even get a chance to grab my old school tape**
>
> **Mad with no music but happy 'cause I'm free**
> **And the streets to a player is the place to be**
> **Got a knot in my pocket weighin' at least a grand**
> **Gold on my neck my pistol's close at hand**
>
> **I'm a self-made monster of the city streets**
> **Remotely controlled by hard hip-hop beats**
> **But just livin' in the city is a serious task**
> **Didn't know what the cops wanted**
> **Didn't have the time to ask**
> **Word.**

I'm telling a story about a guy on the run from the cops, waking up
one day in Los Angeles, going to the County, hitting the streets, and
then getting into a shootout.

I didn't labor over the lyrics. I didn't think this was going to be some
kind of long-lasting or influential record. I was just trying to knock out
a cool B-Side. Nowadays people say that record is the origin of a whole
genre; they trace everything from Tupac to Biggie to Eminem to "6 in
the Mornin'." I didn't call it "gangsta" or "hardcore." To me it was just
the life I was living. If anyone asked me at the time, I called it "reality
rap." Later, when N.W.A. came out, they said explicitly that we're a
gang called "Niggaz With Attitude." And once they dropped the word
"gang," the journalists and the music industry gave the whole, harder-

edged West Coast style the name "gangsta" rap. To me the labels hardly matter: Anytime you say you're solving your problems with a pistol, sure, that's gangsta.

Up to that point—from a national perspective, at least—hip-hop had been all about New York. In the beginning, of course, the influential rappers had all come out of the Bronx, then Harlem, then Queens— they had their New York style. They'd made the blueprint, showed the rest of us how it was done. Mostly, if you listen to the earliest hip-hop, cats were talking about parties, girls. If they were dropping science in a harder way, it was nothing really violent—or it was more subtle. Like in "The Message," when Melle Mel says, "Don't push me, 'cause I'm close to the edge." He doesn't say, "Yo, I'm about to pick up a 9mm and body some niggas." Nobody had dared make anything that violent yet.

I don't know if there was a sense that it wasn't *allowed* but, at the very least, it hadn't been tried. Almost as soon as the label dropped "Dog'n the Wax," we got word that the clubs were heavily spinning the B-Side "6 in the Mornin'." Unknown DJ and I knew pretty quickly that the record was going to be a hit, that people in the street were feeling it. But I figured it would definitely remain underground.

The label sent me up to the Bay Area to play at the Fillmore, and on the strength of that one song, I had the whole Fillmore sold out to see me.

It blew my mind. Everyone liked the crime shit. If you listen to "You Don't Quit" and "Dog'n the Wax," those aren't crime rhymes. They sound much more like something L.L. would do. But at the Fillmore, people were bugging out to that sound. A lightbulb went off: I realized that a lot of people were feeling that crime-story rap, and they probably would be for a long, long time.

THERE WAS SO MUCH hip-hop talent bubbling underneath the surface in Los Angeles. L.A. definitely wanted to be on the map. There was already a rapper named Toddy Tee making some noise in L.A. Not too many people give him props today, but for me, he was a trailblazer. Toddy Tee was more of a comedic rapper who would take other people's records and do parodies. He'd take Whodini's "The Freaks Come Out at Night" and turn it into a record about crackheads. He had a record called "Batter Ram," about the police tank that was running and destroying dope houses in the hood. Toddy Tee had a lot to do with making records totally street, just singing to the 'hood about that whole underground crime thing that was already bubbling up in L.A.

So I took that gangster inspiration of Schoolly D, some of the L.A. flavor of Toddy Tee, and I guess I took it to another level. I said, "I can tell these street stories, tell these crime adventures and do it *my* way—do it as Ice-T."

Between me coming out, and then a little later, N.W.A. and Compton's Most Wanted, we quickly became 'hood heroes. I'd run into street cats and they'd say, "Yo, Ice! Say our name in a record! Rep the 60s!"

Because, let's be honest: A rapper is nothing more than a glorified cheerleader. You're always reppin' something: Bad Boy, Death Row, Dip Set, G-Unit. It's a kind of cheerleading. But because there were so many inter-set beefs in L.A., I always made sure to rep the whole West. *Yo,* I said, *I'm going for it all.* I'll take the whole California. I'm not going to alienate my fans by claiming a certain area. I'll represent the whole West Coast player life.

The bangers I knew were always asking me to rep them in my rhymes—but shouting out Hoover or Harlem or Rollin' 60s? Hell no. I wasn't coming out yelling "C-C-C-Crip!" or "Fuck a Brim!" like I did in those early rhymes I wrote in high school. My audience for those rhymes was all my Crips homeys anyway.

In fact, when I dropped my first records and did my first larger shows like the one at the Fillmore, people that didn't know me used to have these big debates about what neighborhood I was from.

"Yo, Ice is Blood."

"No, Ice is Crip."

"No, you seen them red-and-white Nikes he had on?"

I would always play the middle. Yeah, I sometimes wore *red.* Of course, I did that intentionally. I wanted *all* of L.A. I didn't want to polarize the city. When I started, you didn't claim gang affiliation on a record or in a live show. That shit was no joke. It was still way too dangerous to claim. When I was coming out as an artist, I wasn't about to claim no particular gang and have them other motherfuckers from an opposing set show up at my show and try to kill somebody.

Sure, we had the look. People knew the world we came from. But I wasn't throwing up sets with my hands or the C-Walk—Crip Walk. All that was around us but you didn't try to claim it. You didn't put all that out front in your musical performance.

Years later, after the gang summit and the truce of '92, it became much safer to claim. The gangs of L.A. are still deep but they tend not to bang as hard on sight. You can have Bloods and Crips in the same proximity nowadays and they won't fight unless there's some personal beef between dudes. They've slowed it down a lot. Back in the day, it was *on sight*. You saw an enemy, you'd just take off on him. And given that level of violence and volatility, I didn't see how it would be an advantage to put specifics of gangster life front-and-center in my music.

FLASH FORWARD A FEW YEARS to the situation with Snoop on Death Row. I don't think it would have been possible for someone like Snoop and Suge to have worked together five or six years prior to when they started. People outside the gang world don't understand the degree of politics that went into Snoop linking with Suge. There were lots of raised eyebrows. Because Snoop's a Crip with 21st Street Insanes from Long Beach, and Suge Knight—well, he's not a Blood, but he's strongly connected to the Mob Pirus. When I first started making records, that situation would not have been allowed. It wouldn't have been tolerated for a cat from 21st Street Insanes and a cat from Mob Pirus to work together making music. The Insane and Pirus shotcallers would have squashed it right away. By the time Snoop got involved with Death Row, in fact, the Crips was banging so hard on *other* Crips, they wasn't even worried about no Bloods. But trust me, Snoop and his boys were getting questioned left and right for being with Suge.

I was reppin' the crime side of it, but it wasn't to anybody's advantage to put all that gang content into any of my music. My first rapping partner wasn't a Crip, wasn't a Blood—he was a Mexican. Kid Frost was an *ése,* and in L.A. the *éses* and the blacks clicked together—except in prison because that's a whole different tribal situation: The Northern and Southern Mexicans are even at war in the California State pens. But in L.A., we grew up on the streets close to the Mexicans and, by and large, it's been all good. At least, within hip-hop, it's like the blacks and Puerto Ricans in New York. A lot of Puerto Ricans were important rappers, DJs, graffiti artists, and break-dancers in the early stages of Bronx hip-hop. It's the same with the Mexicans in the L.A. hip-hop scene. They got nothing but love from the brothers.

IT WAS ONE NIGHT, in The Radio, that I created my own Black–Mexican love story. My little cameo in the early hip-hop film *Breakin'* was shot at The Radio. For the film, they'd converted the place into a club called the Radio-Tron.

That's where I spotted Darlene Ortiz. She was this Mexican chick in a tight dress with a body that was simply *crazy:* She looked like she'd been dreamed up by one of those sex-crazed cartoonists who used to airbrush pinup girls on the fuselages of World War II bombers.

People are always fascinated with the bodies of the women I've had relationships with—Adrienne, Darlene, and now my wife, Coco. Okay: It's not too complicated, if this is the type of female you like, then you're going to search them out. Russell Simmons likes tall women, so all his girls are going to look like six-foot, paper-thin models. I like smaller, more athletic-looking chicks. Pretty faces, tiny waists, big round booties. Darlene fit that type to a T.

She's from Riverside, California, so being in The Radio in L.A. was like an out-of-town trip for her. I was mesmerized by her. She was dancing in the club, real sexy. I could tell this was a girl who liked to be noticed.

I walked up to her and hit her with my opening line:

"Would you like to be on an album cover?"

Now, at the time I had no record deal. I had no plans on getting a record deal in the near future.

But it's funny how words—even fly-ass player words—can manifest into reality. Because, of course, Darlene—and especially her body—ended up being on all my early album covers.

We got together, fell in love. For years we had a lockdown good thing. But as I developed, the music business started to spread me out. I had to travel all the time, do interviews, stay out of town for weeks. When we had our son, Ice Tracy Marrow—we all call him Little Ice— that locked Darlene into the house at the very time I needed to spread out.

Looking back on things, I realize that I was like a lot of men—I was not mentally ready for marriage. I don't think most men are ready for the whole trip until they get *out* of their thirties.

Darlene and I were passionate and big dreamers. We were just like a lot of kids at that stage. We all get into romantic dreams; we all think it's going to be forever. That's one of the first things that comes out of young people's mouths when they're in love. *Forever.* And that's cool, it's all good—until you get old enough to realize what forever is.

WHEN I FIRST BROKE IN, that was a great era in the L.A. music scene. Things were popping off all around town. Coolio was coming out with his little clique. There was WC, who used to beat-box for Clientele, part of the World Class Wreckin' Cru. Me and WC have been close friends for years. He's got a record called "Pay Your Dues," where he says, "Thanks to Ice-T, I got my foot in the door." I knew Ice Cube—we became friends; he was a young brother with a lot of charisma who used to come to our shows. He had a group called C.I.A., and they used to do shows at Dr. Dre's parties. He was still raw back then, but once he came out with N.W.A., Cube was a full-blown *beast.* He was a monster at that time. By the time we heard him rhyming with N.W.A., I don't think anyone in L.A. could fuck with Cube.

A crew started to form around me. When you're coming out of L.A. there's a lot of groups and people that are trying to get put on. So you tended to form these alliances and networks. That's how the Rhyme Syndicate was formed. Everlast, later to gain fame with House of Pain, was down with us. Coolio and WC got down with us. And I linked up with Kid Frost. We formed a tight bond and we started doing shows to- gether.

I had my indie records making their noise on the L.A. scene, but I was still strictly known as a local cat. I was still making my home base at The Radio, rocking the mic in the club, introducing various headlining artists who'd come through. First it was the pop and new-wave artists, but there came a point in time when all these New York hip-hop artists started to come to the club like Afrika Islam, Grandmaster Caz, and their crews. This was a big thing to me. These were the original MCs from the Boogie-Down Bronx.

It was a trip for me meeting Grandmaster Caz, the influential MC from the Cold Crush Brothers. And to me, one of the great lyricists in hip-hop history. Afrika Islam was another beast; he was the DJ for the Rock Steady Crew. He was so tight with the pioneering DJ Afrika Bambaataa that his nickname was the "Son of Bambaataa." Islam was also the president of the Zulu Nation. To those of us in L.A. who knew about hip-hop, these cats were legendary. We weren't under any illusions about the West being the best. No, we knew that these Bronx dudes were the real deal.

Here's the funny part: When they met me, both Caz and Islam were tripping off why I wanted to rap.

"Why are you trying to do this, Ice?"

"I'm just trying to get into the game, player," I said. "I'm just trying to get what you got."

"But why the fuck you wanna rap, man?" Caz said. "You already ballin'!"

It was kind of strange: I wanted the level of respect they had in the music community, but they wanted to be making the kind of paper I was already making. They were street cats and could see it just by looking at me. From years in the hustling game, I had more money than *any* of the rappers. I already had all the fly designer gear, the custom-made jewelry, drove any European sports car I wanted. It's hard to imagine it today—given that guys like Jay-Z and Puffy are on the Forbes list of wealthiest businessmen, flying around the world on their private jets— but back in the day, the average drug dealer, pimp, and hustler was pulling in *way* more money than any rapper could imagine making.

So Grandmaster Caz and Afrika Islam were both staring at me like I was nuts for even wanting to pick up the mic.

"Yo, what the fuck is the *matter* with you, Ice?"

Sure, we came from different worlds.

They were intrigued with me; I was intrigued with them.

I especially clicked with Islam. Talking to him at the club, I knew I would have to get my act together and make the trip to his hometown. L.A. was trying to put its own stamp on hip-hop, but you couldn't claim to be serious about the rap game without taking it to New York. To me, being a rapper in L.A. and never gaining acceptance in New York was essentially like not being a rapper at all. New York was the Mecca.

I told Iz, "When I get a record together, I want to come out to New York. Can you help me get on?"

"Bet," he said.

By the time I had "6 in the Mornin'" on wax, and it was making some noise up and down the West Coast, I sent a box of vinyl to Afrika Islam.

"Iz, can you get it spun?" I said.

"Nobody's gonna spin it, Ice," Iz told me. "Not unless you come out here to push it."

So I bought myself a cheap ticket on PEOPLExpress Airlines and got myself out to New York. Soon as I got there, Islam told me the good news: They were playing my record in various clubs and jams around New York.

It was a different-sounding record to New York cats. They were a tough audience to please, but for some reason they were feeling the hardness of that record. They didn't necessarily like my other records, they didn't like the faster party stuff, but they liked that edgy B-Side.

When I touched down in New York, it was the cusp of the second wave of hip-hop. Right after the original old-school cats started to fade. The younger generation like Beastie Boys, Run-DMC, and LL Cool J had come out. This was still before Public Enemy and Eric B. and Rakim hit the scene.

Islam was able to introduce me to Red Alert and Chuck Chillout and Scott "La Rock"—all the big-time DJs in New York who could make or break a record just by putting it into their rotation. All of them liked "6 in the Mornin'" and they started to spin it.

When I came out to New York to push my record, Islam told me he wanted to get me on a track with Melle Mel, on a little label called Posse Records. Just being able to record with Melle Mel—the powerhouse lyricist in Grandmaster Flash's Furious Five—are you kidding me? Now my ego was at an all-time high. I was making the grade. Rolling with the big dogs. To me, these New York cats were on another level.

Grandmaster Caz is definitely charismatic as hell. Melle Mel is a monster lyrically. These cats would write their rhymes right in the studio while the track was playing. On the spur of the moment, they'd pull all this complex poetry out of thin air, just sit down and write the rhyme they were about to spit. I'd never done that. I'd never *seen* anybody do that. They were pressure players. I had to get better if I wanted to be on their level. But then these cats had been rapping for ten years by the time I met them. This is what they did full-time.

I had enough confidence to know I had my own place in the hip-hop game. I had a different story to tell. See, in hip-hop, it's all about your content. I had unique content. I didn't sound like I was mimicking anyone else. I was willing to push the edge. I'd do nasty raps. Violent raps. Real street-reality-based rhymes like "6 in the Mornin'."

I pushed the boundaries. Nobody had said "nigga," "ho," or "muthafucka" on wax before I did. And a lot of subjects and areas that I explored, guys like Grandmaster Caz and Melle Mel—as talented as they were—wouldn't touch. I never thought I could out-rap any of the New York legends, but I was a bit more thought-provoking than the other rappers in the game. There was nobody else rapping about the streets the way that I did.

In fact, that was the main question about me: Could a guy base an entire a career around something so hard and so negative?

EVERYTHING THAT KICKED OFF for me next was through Afrika Islam's connections. Through Iz I met this cat Ralph Cooper who had a connect with Seymour Stein up at Sire Records. Now we were talking a major label, part of the Warner Bros. empire. Up till this point, I'd just been recording for small indie labels, mostly selling records out of mom-and-pop stores.

Word comes down that Seymour Stein wants to do a hip-hop compilation album, and he's already decided on the artists. He wants to use Grandmaster Caz, Melle Mel, Donald D, Bronx Style Bob, and me. Most of these guys already had contractual obligations. Caz had a record deal with Tuff City. Mel was still locked down on Sugar Hill. Donald D had some problems with his label—so I was the only rapper on the compilation who had some experience recording and didn't have the ball-and-chain of legal paperwork that would fuck up any deal.

So I got my major label deal by default—like a comedy of errors: everybody else had some issues and I was the last man standing. Seymour didn't understand that there was this West Coast–East Coast thing, didn't understand that the "authentic" rappers were all from New York and supposedly you couldn't rap if you were from L.A.

"Okay," he said. "I'll take Ice-T."

Seymour Stein is a music industry heavyweight, known as one of the real A&R geniuses in the Rock and Roll Hall of Fame. Seymour's a Jewish cat from Brooklyn with mad game; he signed The Ramones, The Pretenders, Madonna. He's cut from that cloth of the old-time music executives like Clive Davis, but he's way more eccentric than Clive. Clive would go out and sign Whitney Houston and Alicia Keyes; Seymour would go take a chance on the Talking Heads. Just a little more bizarre, a bit more avant-garde, more of an edgy cat.

After I heard that he picked me, I went up to his office with Islam.

"Ice-T!" Seymour said, shaking my hand and staring at me a little too long.

"Hey, how you doing, Seymour?"

"You know, Ice, you have the most beautiful eyes."

I was glancing at Islam, kind of backing away. Moving slowly back toward the door. Islam whispered, "Be cool, man, be cool." Iz was trying to tell me, *This crazy-ass dude's got the money.*

The weirdest thing was the way Seymour was dancing around his office in his socks. And he was blasting some happy-sounding Caribbean music.

"Ice-T, do you understand what this music is?"

"Naw, man."

"This is calypso. Do you know what they're saying? Do you understand calypso?"

"Naw, man. Not really."

"Well, they're talking about the issues in Trinidad. They're talking about the political and social issues. But they're using a lot of double entendre."

"Okay."

I glanced at Islam again. I mean, coming out the 'hood, I didn't have a clue what this dude Seymour was talking about.

"Just because you don't understand their music doesn't make it any less *valid*. It just means *you* don't understand."

"Okay."

"And the same way I may not understand all of what you're saying in your music doesn't make it less valid. It just means I don't know your issues."

I nodded.

"I might not know your issues but I know what you're trying to do."

Then he told me that he'd listened to my lyrics and he thought I sounded like Bob Dylan.

I knew who Bob Dylan was, of course. I didn't know that much about his music, but I knew Seymour was paying me a big compliment.

"Look, I want you to make this record, and I'm going to give you a forty thousand dollar advance."

That was the cool thing about Seymour Stein. He was the dude who could say, "I'll give you this money and you guys bring me back a record." He didn't want to hold your hand through the whole recording process, or look over your shoulder and give unwanted advice, or have a flunky A&R man in the studio with you telling you how to improve the tracks. He literally wrote us a check for the entire budget of that first album and we walked out the door of his office, ready to roll.

Even back then forty grand wasn't much of a budget, but we didn't give a damn. Iz and me walked out of there and bought SB-12 and 909 drum machines. We made the whole album with those two drum machines. We recorded it in New York and mixed it in one night at Secret Sounds studio. Afrika Islam and me put it all together.

We hired Glen Friedman to shoot the cover. Glen was the photographer who shot all the album covers for Beastie Boys, LL Cool J and, a little later, Public Enemy. So my album had that same look as all the hot rappers, and it just fit into a slot.

But with one big difference in the album art: We intentionally wanted to have a palm tree, a car, and a girl—my girl Darlene—in a bikini. That was the intent. Glen said, "This has to look like California. New York cats aren't driving red convertibles, they don't have palm trees, and when they think Cali, what do they think of? They picture girls in bathing suits."

That shot of Darlene was some of the first skin ever on a hip-hop album cover. Groups like the Ohio Players used to use a lot of sexy shots of girls, but that wasn't being done in the rap game. It got more graphic when we did the album *Power*—we just hit them with her body and an even skimpier bathing suit—like *bang*.

Darlene was up front in my career; she did all my album covers. She wasn't just my girl in real life; she was essential to my image. But understand: I was very much about not having anything fake. If it ain't your girl, don't put her in the video. She's wearing *my* chain with the gun pendant on the album cover. That's *my* car. Maybe I was naïve about this shit, but I didn't know you could lie. I didn't know you could fake. I really didn't believe it was okay—especially with rap. I got a song where I say:

> **I don't rhyme about guns I ain't shot**
> **Hoes I ain't caught**
> **Or shit I ain't bought**
> **The game to me is too fucking deep**
> **If I did I honestly believe**
> **I'd die in my sleep . . .**

To me, coming from that hustler's lifestyle, it was like: Why would you have a model? How fake is that? Why would you have girls in your video that you don't even know? That's fake, brother. Everybody in my videos was my friend. When we shot the "High Rollers" video, I said, "The gats in the promo shots ain't props." And they damn sure weren't.

We all used real money—wasn't no fake cash. It was real. Because I was rapping about real shit.

We weren't trying to sound or look like any established hip-hop acts. We weren't on a hip-hop label like Def Jam. *Rhyme Pays* came out, hit the streets, and with virtually no radio support at all, within the year, it went gold.

I WAS SIGNED to a major label, but it was definitely a rock and pop label. Madonna was the biggest artist Seymour had on his roster, but the bulk of Sire's music was edgier rock like the Talking Heads, Depeche Mode, and the Cure. To be honest, I didn't think I was going to have more than one record, with Seymour or anybody else. I honestly thought it was going to be one-and-done—but what a blast we had taking that ride, you know?

Coming from L.A., stepping into this relatively new forum called hip-hop, shit, to think that you could actually sell half-a-million records—and you weren't getting any radio spins; and you weren't from New York, and you didn't *sound* like you were from New York—frankly, I didn't think it was possible.

Through Afrika Islam, I met Afrika Bambaataa. Bambaataa was one of the trinity of pioneers—alongside Kool Herc and Grandmaster Flash—known for having built this massive following around his parties at the Bronx River housing projects. What interested me most about Bambaataa was that he'd been a gangster, a member of the infamous Black Spades, who'd decided that hip-hop culture was an avenue to steer kids away from the crime, drugs, hopelessness, and negativity of gang life. Bambaataa and Islam taught me the Zulu Nation mantra, which is: we all going in the same direction, so why compete unless one of us is a bitch? Why act like crabs in a barrel? Let's try to build together and help each other.

So that's how Rhyme Syndicate solidified. The core of the Syndicate was Evil E, Hen Gee, DJ Unknown, DJ Aladdin, Everlast, Donald D, Toddy Tee, and Afrika Islam. By 1988 we'd decided to do a collective album—all the songs were aggressive, gangster, or socially conscious—called *Rhyme Syndicate Comin' Through.* To me, the Rhyme Syndicate was about building unity with some of L.A.'s dopest rappers, DJs, and producers—our own attempt to do what Bambaataa had done with Zulu Nation and Soulsonic Force. It was also about letting the East Coast cats know that while we weren't *challenging* them, weren't questioning their originality, we definitely wanted them to know that the West brought something to the game. That's why I said:

> **The East started breakin'**
> **But the West started poppin'**
> **But what does it matter**
> **As long as it's rockin'?**

There was something in the ether in 1987. About the same time we put out *Rhyme Pays,* Eric B. and Rakim put out their debut record, *Paid in Full.* Now *Paid in Full* is a classic, but if you listen to the content, it's not that gangsta—not in terms of the lyrics. But they repped that look, with the big gold chains, repping that hustler look. Rakim's voice sounded so hard without even cursing or getting too graphic; I think the hardest thing Rakim ever said in any of his records was, "I used to roll up / This is a holdup / Ain't nothin' funny / Stop smilin' / Be still, don't nothin' move but the money." That was his little poetic window into being a stickup kid; he didn't harp on it, he just made that little allusion.

But I was the polar opposite. I wasn't alluding to *shit.* I harped on the criminal exploits. That's where I came from in reality, and that's what I expected my music and my performances to reflect.

But I was definitely pushing the envelope, especially for a major label like Sire.

I remember one day when Seymour Stein called me up, sounding kind of perturbed. He said he wanted to talk to me about one of my lyrics. I knew exactly what he was going to say. See, I had a song called "409" on *Rhyme Pays* with a lyric that went, "Guys grab a girl, girls grab a guy, if a guy wants a guy please take it outside."

Seymour quoted that line to me. "Ice," he said, "come on. What's that?"

"Seymour," I said. "Look, I'm straight. Now if I wanted to get on the record and say 'Guys grab a guy,' that would be okay? It would be cool to say I'm gay on a record, but I can't say I'm straight? I'm not saying to go bash no one. I'm just saying, personally, I don't want to see it."

He kept giving me static, saying that journalists and critics would see it as an anti-gay statement. That I'd alienate some potential fans.

So I flipped the script on him.

"What do you think of the record?" I said.

"Well, to be honest, I'm feeling a lot of *tension*."

"What does your daughter think of the record?"

"She loves it."

"You know that tension you're feeling, Seymour? That tension is probably *money*."

And then we hung up. That was the deal with Seymour. He wasn't going to edit nothing. That wasn't his deal. He'd speak his mind. He'd show his concern. But he wouldn't try to control me. We had records like *Sex,* and that song was superedgy back in the late eighties— hip-hop hadn't got nearly as graphic and X-rated as it did ten years later.

IT WAS GREAT CHEMISTRY. Seymour supported us business-wise, but he didn't meddle in the creative side of what we were doing. And we delivered the goods. We put out a string of albums for Warner Bros.: *Rhyme Pays,* then *Power, Freedom of Speech, Original Gangster.* All of them certified gold records.

I was like the king of the world over there at Warner Bros. Of the black artists, the only one who was selling more than me was Prince. As far as the hip-hop went, I was over there pretty much alone, and then Cold Chillin' Records came over to the Warner umbrella. Cold Chillin' had Big Daddy Kane and that's when me and Kane started going out and doing promotional tours.

And eventually Uptown Records came over there as well. I hadn't met Puffy yet—but just like the famous story goes, he was this young, hustling kid running around as a mail clerk for Andre Harrell back then. Benny Medina was my go-to guy at Warner. So Andre was the boss at Uptown and Puffy was working for him. And it was Benny who'd signed Andre to Warner. But a little later it all flipped: Puffy became the man and Benny transitioned into J.Lo's manager. It was crazy but that's the music industry for you. I've had years in the music biz to observe this: Don't get too hung up on working with any one person, because it's like a game of checkers where dudes are hopping over one another all the time, shouting, "King me, motherfucker!" It's checkers, yo. But with a lot of money at stake.

WE HAD SOME CRAZY TIMES in those early days of my rap career. It was a glamorous time. Pretty much the first thing on my agenda was indulging my taste for expensive cars. I had one of the first Ferraris to hit the scene. It was a candy-apple-red Ferrari Mondial convertible. Just gorgeous. I was one of the first cats to drive that exotic shit. Motherfuckers were still low-riding in L.A.

Now I've got to explain something about Flavor Flav. By the time Public Enemy came out, Flav and I were tight. He'd come see me whenever he was on the West Coast and we'd hang out. I was like his surrogate Chuck D. He'd listen to Chuck D when he was in the East and he respected me like I was like a West Coast Chuck D.

This one afternoon Flav showed up at my house in Hollywood, out of control, with those fucking antlers on, honking his car horn. In L.A.

Flav is not an act. That nigga's crazy! Hanging out with Flav is a wild adventure. He'll be rolling, stop his car in the middle of an intersection, jump out and fix his pants and shit while a bunch of cars are honking. Every time he stops the car, there's drama. I always say, "Flavor is a walking event."

He dropped by my house and we decided to roll to Red Lobster. We took two cars: I was in my new Ferrari, Flav and Terminator X were following us in a rented Mustang.

I pulled into this parking structure. I could see in the rearview mirror that Flavor was screaming and waving his arm and doing what he always does, and then the fool smashed right into the back of my brand-new Ferrari.

We all heard the brake light shatter.

It got really quiet and then Terminator X said, "Oh shit, you just wrecked Ice's ride."

All he really did was bust the brake light, he didn't do any structural damage, didn't bend the car. Still, it looked bad.

Flavor gets out of the rental car and for one minute he's transformed back into William Drayton—he's no longer crazy-ass Flavor Flav. He's talking to me like an attorney, in his real voice. "Ice, I am really sorry for this mishap." None of that "Yeeaaaaaah, boyeeeee!" shit.

He took a little piece of the brake light and—word is bond!—he probably still has that shit in his wallet. He carried that brake light for years! Every time I'd see him, in L.A., New York, anywhere, he'd open his wallet and show it to me. And he'd tell everyone within ear shot: "That day was the closest I ever came to death. I really thought Ice was going to kill me for cracking his Ferrari."

I HAD A SONG ON *Rhyme Pays* called "Squeeze the Trigger." And when Dennis Hopper—rest in peace—was finishing up his film *Colors,* which he directed, I got word that they wanted to use "Squeeze the Trigger" in the movie. I said, "That's cool. Can I see the movie first?" It was still a rough cut, no score or soundtrack yet, and the producers set up a screening for us. Dennis showed me the scene where Don Cheadle's character, Rocket, is listening to music, which is where they wanted to put the song.

The movie was nearly finished and I asked, "Hey, do you have a title song yet?"

They said yes they had a song by Rick James called "Colors." It was a funky beat, but it was Rick James wailing, *"Look at all these coloooooors,"* sounding—well, exactly like superfreak Rick James. I knew if they used that Rick James song, it was going to sound corny as hell, especially in a film about gangbanging. They needed something hard. They needed a song that was authentic to the L.A. gangbanging world.

"Naw, man," I said, "Let me hook up a new title song for this piece."

So I went off to write "Colors." Now, there was a song out by King Sun called "Mythological." I thought the song was dope and decided I'd

use it as a kind of format for "Colors." Islam had this little bass line
sample in his Roland machine. We used the beat from "Mythological,"
and I did my own variation of King Sun's flow:

I am a nightmare walking
Psychopath talking
King of the jungle
Just a gangster stalking

I rocked a gangster story to the cadence of "Mythological." It was a
first-person gangbanging story with a line most people remember—
The gangs of L.A. will never die—just multiply . . .

A lot of hip-hop records are made that way: building on what other
brothers are putting out there into the game. It's not considered copy-
ing, unless you don't acknowledge the other artist, but it is more about
"influence." A lot of cats will rhyme to the cadence of another artist's
song that really got under their skin for some reason. The funny thing
about "Colors" is that the trademark sound, this trippy echo that
sounds kind of like church bell on reverb, was something that came out
of a machine by mistake. The engineer hit a wrong button in the echo
machine and said, "Oh shit, let me wipe it clean."

"No," I said. "That's so fucking dope! Put that in the record."

It was random, like amp feedback in some old sixties rock records,
but it was the sound that people remember most about that track. That
weird ringing echoing sound—nothing planned, just a fuck-up that we
left in the final mix.

The thing about that movie—I'll be the first to say it—sure, it was
fake. The story line had the Crips fighting the Mexicans. But to me that
didn't matter too much. A lot of people who get mad at the inauthen-
ticity of *Colors* don't know the backstory of how the movie got made.
Dennis Hopper told me that he wanted to make a movie about gangs,
and the movie studio told him he had to set and shoot it in Chicago.
"Why Chicago?" Hopper said. "We have gangs in L.A."

"We have gangs in L.A.?" an executive said.

Hopper told those studio suits that same year there'd been 367 kids killed—that's how invisible the gang culture still was to even L.A. film executives. If you're in Beverly Hills, you don't know the first thing about what's going on down in South Central and Compton.

Dennis convinced them to make it about gangs in L.A., but when they decided to go in—I guess they heard how real the banging was between the sets and got really, really afraid of portraying the gang world—they intentionally created something fictionalized, like Crips fighting Mexicans, because they didn't dare show the Crips warring with Bloods. They sidestepped the issue, figuring the movie was toxic enough without them pissing off real sets of Crips and Bloods.

If you're from out of town, and you don't really know Watts or Compton, it's not too far off base. Of course, gangbangers pick at that movie like they are picking lint out of fly shit. They'll always say, "Naw, it wasn't like that."

But I've worked on enough film and TV sets to know this: It would be damn near impossible to make a movie play-by-play on how the gang situation was going down in L.A. What *Colors* did is make people around the country aware that there was a serious gang scene in L.A.

I wasn't in the movie—a lot of people think I acted in it, but I just did the title song and the video. We were nominated for an MTV Award for that, too. I think that the song still holds up today. I just cared about keeping the song as real as I could from the gangbangers' perspective. That's all I cared about. The song was more real than the movie, to be honest.

CALL IT UNCOMPROMISING. Call it hardheaded. I thought it was all about "artistic integrity." I decided that I wasn't going to do any radio edits of my songs. I mean, I wasn't getting any radio love anyway. My records *never* got played. So I figured, why should I clean up my lyrics for these suckers?

N.W.A. was raw as fuck—when they topped the *Billboard* album chart, they had to censor the band's full name—but even *they* started making clean radio versions. I refused flat out. I was really on some rebel shit. I wouldn't compromise my artistic principals. The fact that my records sold well—got RIAA-certified gold status—without any air-play and that I was able to earn an income meant, in a sense, that I could afford not to give a fuck. I was real hard. I didn't like going up to radio stations and kissing their ass only to have them still not play my records. I even had a song called "Radio Suckas Never Play Me" with a hook I sampled from Chuck D.

I was making all my money pretty much selling records and touring. Hip-hop was still like that. You could do it on a street level back in the day. Acts like Master P and Geto Boys built these huge, loyal fan bases without radio play, just by doing regional shows and selling their shit on an indie label. Literally selling their tapes out of the trunks of cars and in mom-and-pop record shops. You could get a following out there—but you couldn't be too pop. You had to have a really hard product.

Luke and 2 Live Crew were selling a million copies with each album—and they were selling pretty much all of them down in Florida! It could be done back then. There wasn't an Internet, no file sharing or downloading to kill your store sales. Fans had to buy the record—not even CDs sometimes, it was still cassette tapes, and you had to physi-cally own the product.

My base was always L.A. first and New York second, and Detroit was always my third, then Chicago, then Atlanta—but my stuff moved in all the American cities. Overseas, my stuff was always selling steadily, mostly in Germany—they buy the most records.

It's funny—the more you aim to hit a hardcore 'hood audience, the more the white suburban kids seem to get into your music. They don't especially want to hear pop bullshit, except maybe the really younger crowd and teenage girls. But as I was going out touring, I was seeing al-most all-white crowds at my shows. Here's how it breaks down in hip-hop: When you're doing it in the garage and small clubs, it's almost all black kids. But once you make it to arenas and bigger venues, it be-comes almost all white kids. I learned real quickly to adjust my racial perspective, especially when I toured out of the country and saw lots of white kids who idolized me and dug my words. I'd see them dressed all in the Raiders gear that they saw in my videos. That made me step back as an artist and say, "Maybe I don't know everything."

For me, it's why you see progression in music, whether it's the Beatles or hardcore hip-hop; part of that transformation is that groups start to travel, start to grow as artists, start to change their perspectives.

When we'd to go Germany or Italy or Japan, these kids used to line up to take pictures of my sneakers. It wasn't enough for them to see your look; they needed to have a blueprint. At some of these shows, these suburban kids would look like they were from L.A. I remember one time I was playing in Memphis, and I saw this kid in the crowd who had on a khaki shirt that said, ROLLIN' 60S CRIPS COLORS. As in *Colors*— the movie.

Shit. I was like—*What the fuck does this white kid know about the Rollin' 60s?* Dennis Hopper's flick had a lot to do with spreading that gangsta "chic." You can't believe how many people would hit us up with that gang sign that the Mexican kid did in the movie, which was made up—but these kids all over the Midwest copied it, thinking that made them look badass. You start to realize that this gang shit is soaking in. You'd even start seeing the Crip Walk done in places that had never seen a real live Crip. That bugged me out. Some kid from a nice suburb with a mom, dad, dog, and two-car garage tying a bandanna around his head and claiming a set that's three thousand miles away from his house. *Okay, son . . . you're Eight-Trey Gangsta and you're in fuckin' Kentucky!*

It was one thing when the fans just had our album covers, but once *Yo! MTV Raps* hit, the kids emulated everything we were doing in the videos. A lot of them got obsessed with the mimicry. Rappers were often yelling at the kids saying, "Yo, don't be us, be you!" But you can't preach to a fan who's set on living out a fantasy life because he thinks it's cool.

I used to have all these white kids from Newport Beach come up to my house in Hollywood and hang out with all my gangbanger friends from South Central. That was a trip. See, the bangers got along with the white boys because the white boys were surfers. Straight-up. They didn't front like they were hip-hoppers, or pretend to be gangsters. They'd all sit around smoking and I'd hear my hustler friends getting at them, "Just be a surfer, man. That's who you are, ya dig? Don't come up here trying to look like me. You know, your weed is better than my weed anyway, so we cool!"

That's basically the gangster code. Just be yourself. Just be you, dog. The easiest way to get your card plucked around a gangster is to be a fake. If we feel like you're trying too hard, if you're trying to act like you're from the street, you're in trouble.

9.

CHUCK D ONCE SAID, "Ice-T is the only person who does things that completely *jeopardize* his career just to stay awake." Once I get something going well, I'll risk fucking it up just for the action. I'm not a cat to stay on cruise control. I hate the idea of being in a comfortable groove. I'll have my rap game going good, and say fuck it, now I'll do a hard rock record. I'll get that rock thing going good and say, fuck it, now, I'm gonna act.

No, I never think about it as jeopardizing my career. That's just how I'm cut. Even in school, I always loved going against the grain. I loved doing shit that everyone told me not to do. Right now, I'm thinking I might branch out into standup comedy. Who knows? I like to keep shit moving. Chuck could be right . . . maybe I do it to keep myself awake.

I've always been theatrical, and ever since my first music video for "I'm Your Pusher," I felt I could hold my own in front of a camera. We came up with this concept for the song, with the music becoming the "dope." We were acting like drug dealers on the street, but we were pushing our outlawed music. "I'm Your Pusher" got a little airplay because I had a singing hook. But after I realized how easy getting airplay was, I intentionally never did it again. I never used a singing hook in any of my rap records.

Acting was foreign territory for those of us in the hip-hop game. In their video for "Follow the Leader," Eric B and Rakim took it up a notch with acting, and other rappers were doing it, too—the music video became more skits. Guys like Kurtis Blow and Run-DMC had played themselves in *Krush Groove* and *Tougher Than Leather.* But nobody had done any serious acting. Probably because no serious directors or producers were looking at rappers.

I've always liked to be on the cutting edge. I liked that I was the first to do shit. First to bring hardcore cursing to a rap record. First to really rap about the L.A. gangster life. But I never actually dreamed I'd become the first rapper to get a starring role in a major Hollywood movie.

When the opportunity knocked, to be honest, I thought it was a bullet in my head. For real. *Krush Groove* and *Tougher Than Leather* had come out, but these were rap movies.

It's funny how my acting career got started. I was in this club at the same time as Mario Van Peebles. Mario said he overheard me talking shit in the bathroom—I don't remember this exactly, but apparently I was telling someone: "The problem is, if they could put me under a microscope and find one molecule of me that *gave* a fuck, then they'd have a chance."

Mario apparently heard that and he said on the spot, "Okay, whoever said that is going to be the star of my next movie." That movie would be *New Jack City.* Then he figured out it was me, and he came over and found me at the other side of the club.

"Ice," he said, "I've got a movie role for you."

I was busy talking to some chicks so I figured that was just bullshit he was spitting to be introduced to the girls. So I introduced them, nodding, but Mario kept staring at me.

"No, I'm serious, Ice. Here's my number, call me tomorrow."

"Yeah," I said, still brushing him off.

"Player, I've got a movie set up at Warner Brothers. Call me tomorrow and let's talk about it. If you're into it, we'll get you the script."

The next day I called his number, and it was serious business.

"Ice, listen. This role is yours if you want it."

"What are you talking about, Mario?"

"Just come down to Warner today."

I drove to Warner Bros., sat down in Mario's office, and they gave me the script.

"What's the character's name?"

"Scottie. Scottie Appleton."

Just skimming through the script, I could see that my character was damn near on every page. "Yo, Mario, this is a starring role—I can't do it."

"Yes, you can."

"Who else you got for the picture?"

"Let's see. . . . We got Chris Rock," he said. "We got Wesley Snipes . . ."

Those are box office names *now,* especially Chris, but at the time they were not big movie stars. Wesley had only done one film, *Major League,* and Chris was known for being a player on *Saturday Night Live,* certainly not the huge box-office draw he is now.

I took the script home and read it closely. Didn't take me more than a page or two to grasp who the character Scottie Appleton was.

"This dude is a *cop*! What the fuck? They want me to play a cop? And hold up. What's this shit? He's got dreadlocks!" At the time, I was still rocking a perm. I still looked like a straight-up West Coast pimp. I couldn't picture myself playing a New York dude in dreads.

Mario had a producing partner named George Jackson, and George started leaning on me. "Ice, you can do this. You can pull this off, we need you."

They'd done their research, saying they had a movie that needed young black actors, and there weren't that many bankable black actors under thirty years old. Damn near none. So they made what was then a risky decision: Maybe some of these rappers and R&B singers, with their existing fan bases, will translate into box office.

That's why in *New Jack City* you see Christopher Williams, Teddy Riley, Flavor Flav, Troop. It was a form of hedging their bets. They decided to cast the movie using musicians whose careers were hot, give it a hot soundtrack; that way, if they couldn't sell the movie, they could make their investment back on the soundtrack alone.

I'm usually pretty self-assured, make decisions quickly, and don't question myself. Most aspects of my career, I've trusted my gut instinct alone. But this movie role had me confused as fuck. I didn't know what to do. I put off giving Mario an answer for as long as I could.

How could I take the role of a cop? I'd been a criminal. I'd been representing the criminal life in my music. How could I flip the script now and play Jake on screen? What would my core fans—what would my closest friends—think of that switch? I started to survey all the people around me, people whose opinion I trusted most.

"Yo, I got offered this movie role," I said over and over. "But here's the thing: they want me to be the *man*."

I thought my old crime partners might start laughing. Or snap my head off. But they all had the same response. They got these puppy faces, turned real quiet for moment, then asked me, "Word? Ice, could I be in the movie?"

I checked with the hardest cats I knew, my crime partners who were behind those big walls. And even cats locked up in the pen weren't fazed by the fact I'd be playing an undercover cop.

"Dig, Ice," they said. "If I was out on the street, you think I could be in the movie?"

That shocked me, to be honest. None of them were tripping on me playing police. Their reaction was more like the excitement of little kids who found out one of their buddies won free tickets to the Super Bowl.

"Nigga, you made it! You get to be in a movie!"

All the girls I knew in the 'hood were looking at it a little differently. They saw it as a major responsibility. "Ice, baby, you better do this. You better take this opportunity, because if you do the movie, you're going to keep it real. You ain't like these other motherfuckers who get over and stop talkin' about shit."

So after that consensus. I jumped. I called Mario and told him, yeah, I'd play the part of the undercover narc in his movie.

———

WHEN WE STARTED SHOOTING *New Jack,* a lot of times I found myself switching between being an actor and a technical consultant. Wesley was constantly asking me for advice. He knew I was a real street cat. "Shit," he'd say, "I got Ice here—we gonna do this correct!"

A lot of times it was the lingo—getting the street slang up-to-date—or a subtle gesture, basically how we would roll on the street. Everybody in the movie knew what they were doing as actors. No one was off-beat. Sometimes they needed a little help with the swagger.

The trick I learned is that when you're making a movie—and later on doing television—it's got to feel real but not *be* real. The art is to be able to eliminate the trivial, repetitive details of reality for the sake of telling the story. For instance, you can't solve a crime every week in forty-two minutes like we do on *Law & Order.* You have to accelerate the pace. That's why when you see me playing Fin on *SVU,* damn near every time I pick up the phone or get handed a piece of paper—*Boom*—the answer is there: "Liv, the DNA results just came in. It's a match." Come on, the answer is never that easy in real life. But we have to sacrifice the mundane reality in order to get the story's pacing right.

I knew Mario wasn't trying to make a documentary about the drug game. There are a lot of details that we put into *New Jack* for excitement and drama, but the film was as close to real as we could make it. The basis of the story was true: There really were crews who took over entire housing projects in New York City, crews who had teams of naked chicks up in fortified apartments cooking that powder into rock. In the movie, we just had sexier girls; flyer-looking lawyers; hipper-talking cops.

New Jack was a hell of a shooting experience. But I won't front. Most of us were really nervous. Judd Nelson was a lifesaver. He was an actor with real established credibility and he told me, "Yo, everybody fucks up. If you're worrying about fucking up, you're not gonna be able to do the scene. Just do it. Don't trip." He really relaxed guys like me and Chris who hadn't been in films before.

The part of Gee Money was famously played by Allen Payne, who'd been on *The Cosby Show,* and now stars on *House of Payne.* What people don't know is that Gee Money was originally played by Oran "Juice" Jones, who had the hit "Walkin' in the Rain." We were doing our daily read-throughs of the script. Everything was going smooth, and one day we came in and Oran was gone—just vanished—and Allen Payne was standing there, wearing all the same clothes, same Gee Money jewelry, reading like he'd been there every day. Chris Rock and I looked at each other like "What the fuck just happened?"

Since Chris and I had a lot of lines together, and we were buddies in the movie, we quickly became friends in real life. That day, after they switched Juice and we knew he got fired, when we finished the read-through, they said, "Okay, Ice, Chris, that's a wrap. You guys can go home."

Both me and Chris, in unison, shouted: "No, we'll just stay! We'll *stay.* We don't want to leave. We'll stay until everybody's done for the day."

Then Chris turned to me and whispered: "Hell *no*! I know they got that nigga Sinbad downstairs running through my lines in the script."

"Goddamnit," I said, "They probably got Chuck D down there with a dread wig on. I'm not fuckin' leaving!"

Me and Chris and Wesley remain good friends today. I haven't seen Judd in a minute—but we're all kind of like alumni. We cut our teeth as actors in that film. Almost all of us look at *New Jack City* as being the breakout role of our acting careers.

People still stop me in the street and say "New Jack City!" or "Scotty!" They still walk up to Wesley and shout, "Nino Brown!" in his face. And as much success as Chris has since had with his groundbreaking standup concerts and hit movies, people will still call him "Pookie!" For a relatively small movie, it had a big impact. Of course, we didn't think about that during principal photography. Nobody ever thinks that their very first movie will still hold water twenty-five years later.

New Jack City, along with *Scarface* and *King of New York*, had the biggest impact of any movie within the rap game. Decades later, you still see the ripples. You've still got cats rhyming about Nino Brown. You've got Lil' Wayne—whose real last name is Carter—calling his album *The Carter*, after the housing project in the movie.

The first few days on location was a pretty daunting experience. You start seeing your daily scenes in the rushes, and those images are *raw.*

My parents, Solomon and Alice Marrow

My red fire engine, my first car

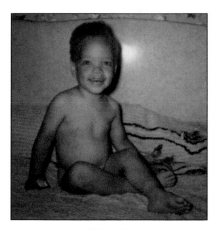

Baby pic

My Crenshaw High School yearbook photo

Rhyme Syndicate N.Y. (from left: Evil E, Beatmaster V, me, Randy Mac, Busy B, Melle Mel, Melvin Bennett, Sean E. Sean, Donald D)

Harry O, Nat the Cat, me, Franzell

Rhyme Syndicate (at my left, Donald D and Hen-Gee)

Body Count on tour (from left: Sean E. Mac, Vincent Price, O.T., me, Ernie C, D-Roc, Sean E. Sean)

On stage with Snoop Dogg at the Apollo

Rocking the mic at VH1's Hip Hop Hono (2005)

On tour with Lil Ice

Live in Miami

A fan's tattoo

Me with a tattooed fan

Me and Coco at the Masters Players Ball, Arlington, Texas (from left: Minister Seamore, Archbishop Don Magic Juan, Fillmore Slim)

West Side: Backstage with Ice Cube in Detroit

Me and my colleagues from *Law & Order: SVU* and *CI* (from left: Richard Belzer, Jeff Goldblum, Mariska Hargitay)

On the set of *Law & Order: SVU* with Chris Meloni

Me and Dick Wolf, producer of the *Law & Order* franchise

Power couples: Chris and Malaak Rock, Ice-T and Coco. Chris Rock and I have been friends since we starred in *New Jack City*.

Me, Coco, and Snoop Dogg at the Comedy Central roast for Flavor Flav

Joking around with Muhammad Ali

Me and Don King

Me and Iron Mike Tyson

Me, Diddy, and Quincy Jones. I won a Grammy Award for the Best Rap Performance by a Duo or Group for Quincy Jones's *Back on the Block* (1989).

"Imagine me shaking hands with the mayor."

Me with New York City mayor Michael Bloomberg

The moment I met Coco, introduced by Rick Ricardo, one of my player buddies

Our wedding photo

Mr. & Mrs. Ice

On the red carpet with Coco

Stepping out

"A successful marriage is built on the realization that the other person has your back no matter what."

Chilling with Baby Ice

Family pic (my grandson, Elijah; my daughter, LeTesha; and Lil Ice)

Rocking the mic at the New Ritz, New York City (1992)

Original Gangsta pic

At the Tunnel nightclub, New York City (1992)

Keepin' it player in pink

Classic O.G.

On the red carpet for VH1's Hip Hop Honors (2005)

Monte Carlo

You don't have the benefit of music, effects or editing tricks, so you've got to imagine the potential of how this scene will fit in the finished movie. Honestly, while we were filming *New Jack,* I didn't ever think I pulled it off. Even after we wrapped, I didn't think I *did* it.

That made me pretty nervous and unsettled. Then I went to see the movie when it first opened, not at some red-carpet premiere, but just a regular screening at Grauman's Chinese Theatre in Hollywood. Bought a ticket, some popcorn and a soda like everyone else. And then I sat in the rear of the theater—lay back in the cut—behind some guys who looked like they were from the streets. My first moment on screen, they started heckling me.

"Aw shit, look at Ice-T in that fuckin' hat."

"Motherfucker looks stupid in them dreads . . ."

But about ten or fifteen minutes into the movie, these same dudes were calling me "Scotty," not "Ice-T."

"Don't do it, Scotty!"

And I bust out laughing.

That's when I said, Oh shit. *I did it.* I made them believe in the character. I never went up to say hi to these dudes who'd been heckling me. I just wanted to get a sense of how a *real* audience would react.

Funny thing is, I'd fought Mario and the producers on how they wanted me to look. They wanted Scotty to have dreads and wear hats and shit. They said one of the reasons they insisted on me having dreadlocks is this: "You've got an existing image; you can't look like Ice-T. Everyone knows Ice-T. We have to break that, give you another vibe, otherwise the audience won't allow you to be the character." That was a great lesson about acting, and it worked.

At the time, the movie created a lot of controversy. It got great reviews from critics like Roger Ebert. But there was major static, too. People don't remember this much today, but at the time, there was a lot of controversy surrounding *New Jack City.*

The film came out about six months before John Singleton's *Boyz in the Hood* and, for a time at least, there was a sense that these " 'hood movies" were going to create a wave of rioting. That black folks couldn't see an action-packed movie about their own lives without going buck-wild. True, there were some disturbances and violence when our movie opened in big cities like New York, Los Angeles, Chicago, and Detroit.

But if you check the facts, only ten of the approximately eight hundred theaters screening the film experienced problems. The violence did get a lot of media play, especially after one screening in Brooklyn, where some dudes from rival housing projects busted shots at each other, killing one man and wounding a woman. Actually the most widely reported incident occurred in Westwood Village in Los Angeles. Mann's Theater sold out tickets for the film's opening night and a mob of pissed-off kids, frustrated that they couldn't get inside, started smashing store windows and vandalizing cars.

To me, the idea that the content of *New Jack City* had these kids wilding out is total bullshit. If a dude is going to shoot another dude at the movies, that's been in his heart *long* before he sits down in the fucking theater. And more than likely, they already have some existing beef.

The onscreen violence in *New Jack City* was much more realistic—much less of a cartoonish, shoot-'em-up kind that was in a lot of Sly Stallone, Arnold Schwarzenegger, or Bruce Willis movies. And if you go back and watch it today, *New Jack* was one of the earliest, strongest *anti*-drug movies. In fact, it was almost preachy and heavy handed in its anti-drug message. One of my major scenes has Scotty saying: "A drug dealer is the *worst* kind of brother. He won't sell it to his sister. He won't sell it to his mother, but he'll sell it to one of his boys on the street."

New Jack City was a surprise hit. The movie was shot for just $8 million, and became the highest grossing independent film of 1992, making over $47 million. My check for the gig? I think I got twenty thousand dollars. The funny part is that it led to my next movie role in *Ricochet* with Denzel Washington and John Lithgow.

Second movie—I thought, *Okay, now I got a track record, now I'm gonna get paid.* I went into the producer Joel Silver's office with that swagger.

I didn't have to do a reading or anything. He just offered me the part. (I've been lucky that way: Every movie role I've done was offered to me; I never had to audition or read for it.) But when it came to paying me, I figured I could up my quote.

"Ice," Joel Silver said, "look, you've done exactly *one* movie."

I only got about forty grand, but for much less work—only a handful of scenes. Shooting with Denzel was mad cool. Then, as now, Denzel was the *man* as far as black actors go. There is nobody more respected. And he was the quietest, most down-to-earth cat on the set. I never once felt like I was some rookie rapper and he was the trained actor who could master every role from Othello to street gangster. With Denzel, there was never a problem if I messed up a line. He'd just smile, give me a pound, and we'd do another take.

At one point, when he could see I was really tense, Denzel even took time to come into my trailer and break it down for me.

"Look, Ice," he said. "I started out in TV. I did TV movies. I did *St. Elsewhere.* I did local theater. Nobody starts off in the big leagues. People look at me like I've made it—but, man, I still have a long way to go. Everybody has to come through a door. You're in the door, Ice. Do your best."

It's not going to help the scene if the actor working with you is intimidated. Good actors need another actor's energy to vibe. If all you're vibing is another person's fear and tension, how the hell can you make the scene work?

I couldn't be cast in a scene with Al Pacino and stand there, staring at him, completely starstruck. *My God, it's Al Pacino.* Once the director says "Action!" all that reverence for the big movie star has to fly out the window. If the role says to disrespect him, I have to disrespect him, even though in real life I hold him in high regard. If my role is written that way, then I'm gonna talk to Al Pacino like he's a real piece of shit. And Al Pacino, in his reactions, is going to be egging me on.

Today, I try to relate that same lesson Denzel gave me when I'm on the set of *Law & Order.* We'll get new kids, young actors, and they'll sit in the interrogation room, and I'll see how nervous they are. They're nervous because they don't know their lines; they're nervous that if they fuck up, Dick Wolf will never use them again. I always take them aside and tell them: "Dig, you know what? It's okay to be nervous. I'm not Ice-T here. I'm Fin. I'm supposed to be police—and we're fucking with you. So hell yeah, you're nervous. Use this!"

I don't exactly see myself as a mentor or trailblazer, but I'm proud of whatever role I played in kicking open the door for a generation of hip-hop artists to make that transition to the big screen. Will Smith, Queen Latifah, Common, LL Cool J. 'Pac did some fine roles, and probably would have grown a lot with his acting if he'd lived longer. Today, you've got guys like my man Lord Jamar from Brand Nubian, my friend Chino XL, Ludacris, Method Man—too many rappers to mention have proven they've got the acting chops to make it in feature films.

But among us all there are only two box office draws: Will and Latifah. That's real talk. I'm no box office draw. I may have a bit of TV buzz—I know Dick Wolf respects my game—but to be categorized as one of those A-list Hollywood actors who can get a movie green-lit on your name alone, to negotiate your deal so that your name appears *above* the title, that's real juice. That's clout. Of black male actors from the hip-hop generation, only Will Smith has got it like that.

For the rest of the rappers, yeah, you can be in the movie, get a juicy part, a sizable check, and your own trailer on the set—but don't get it twisted: You ain't the reason folks paid ten bucks and sat their asses down in that multiplex theater.

PART FOUR

FREEDOM OF SPEECH

**"GODDAMN, WHAT A BROTHER GOTTA DO
TO GET A MESSAGE THROUGH
TO THE RED, WHITE, AND BLUE?"**

—"BODY COUNT"

10.

MY FRIENDS ALL KNOW one thing about me: I can never sit still. I have a really low threshold for boredom. It's pretty ironic considering that acting and recording can be such monotonous professions.

Quiet as it's kept, I actually *hate* recording. The only part of rapping that's fun to me is performing live. To get a crowd going buck-wild. Waving their hands in the air. Shouting along to your lyrics. But when you're in the studio, doing take after take, punching in little mistakes in your vocals, that's tedious as fuck.

I hate the time that's required to be a perfectionist in the studio. I like coming in and laying my vocals down quick. I'm not one of those artists that likes to sit in there for two or three days just to make one song. Rev Run said once that he wishes he could write the rap, throw it into the air, and it would end up instantly on the radio so he could hit the road and perform it live. All the work that goes into polishing the record, that's pure tedium. Good producers get off on that. I'm not that dude. I like live performing. There's nothing like standing in front of an insane crowd of twenty or thirty thousand people when they're feeling you.

Back in the day, you had to do shows on a regular basis just to get a record deal. They used to make new artists have a showcase just so all the record executives and "taste-makers" could watch them perform live. Either that, or you'd be an undiscovered artist playing at a little club, and some A&R guy would decide if you could rap live before he even thought about signing you.

These days, all that shit is backward. In the age of YouTube, Facebook, Twitter, and home studios with ProTools, so many artists put their own music out there and start grassroots promotional campaigns before they've ever left their bedroom or garage to perform that shit. Their first time performing live is when they've already become stars; they've got their recording and only later create a live show around themselves.

I'm not saying our generation was *better;* it's just different. People thought MTV changed up the music business, putting the emphasis on the artist's *look* rather than how he sounded; but that's nothing compared to what a forum like YouTube has done. In the documentary I just shot, *The Art of Rap,* I say, "First we were in the audio age, now we're in the video age." You see someone's YouTube clip—some no-name kid who's got a million hits before you've ever heard of them in the mainstream. The whole music game has become much more visually driven than audio. Back in the day, you'd hear a band's song a long time— months and months—before you even knew what they looked like.

I WOULDN'T EXACTLY SAY I was *bored* with the rap game, but by 1989, I wanted to expand my musical horizons. My love for rock didn't start with my band, Body Count. My introduction to rock started when I was living in my aunt's house back in the mid-seventies.

My first cousin, Earl, had already graduated from Dorsey High, but he was hanging around, thinking he was Jimi Hendrix. He was one of the few rocked-out black guys I'd met; he wore a scarf around his head and only listened to KMET and KLOS in L.A.—the two rock stations.

For a while, when I first came to live with my aunt, I had to share a bedroom with him. I was just a kid in junior high, so Earl controlled the radio in the room, playing nonstop classic rock.

I didn't hang with Earl, but just being around him, sharing that bedroom radio, I started to pick out the songs I liked. I had no taste for rock before Cousin Earl. He had his well-worn Jimi Hendrix and Black Sabbath albums; and from listening to the radio I learned about Leon Russell, Mott the Hoople, Blue Oyster Cult, Deep Purple. All the heavy rock bands of that era. If you're saturated with a certain type of music long enough, you'll start to pick out the artists you like. If you worked in an area full of Jamaicans, you're going to listen to reggae so much that eventually you're going to say, "You know, I like that song by Peter Tosh."

So right at the age when my musical taste was forming, thanks to Cousin Earl, I was saturated with the bigger, heavier stuff: Edgar Winter, Led Zeppelin, and Black Sabbath were my favorites. It was kind of cool to know about that shit. Not too many black kids my age knew about the great rock guitarists.

There was one other black rock head at Crenshaw High. Ernie Cunnigan from South Central. We all called him Ernie C. Ernie was a *dedicated* guitar player. He was a real different dude. In the midst of the whole gang culture at Crenshaw—everyone wearing the same uniform of pressed khakis, Chuck Taylors, flying blue rags—Ernie C. would walk around with a Fender guitar strapped over his shoulder like he was constantly on his way to a gig. He did this one concert at Crenshaw, right there in the multipurpose room—*crazy*! He had flash pots he'd made at home; he was rolling around on the stage, playing Peter Frampton songs lick for lick. The audience was all gangbangers, standing around watching him, these Crips who didn't know shit about rock music. But they all respected Ernie C. because of his showmanship and his sheer balls.

Vic Wilson, also known as Beatmaster V, could play the drums, but he got caught up in the drug game more and more until he and Sean E. Sean caught that case for the twenty-six pounds in their crib down in Inglewood.

When I first got my deal with Sire Records, anybody with any musical aptitude gravitated toward me. Ernie and Vic would constantly say, "Ice, you got an album deal. Yo, let's play!"

"No, this is hip-hop. I don't really need a band."

If you go back and check my early recordings, I always had a rock influence in my rap records. On my first album, *Rhyme Pays,* for the title song I used the hook from Black Sabbath's "War Pigs." I let Beatmaster V play live drums over the sample. I get a lot of haters who think I somehow jumped on the rock bandwagon, that my rock 'n' roll band was a marketing gimmick, but if I didn't really love it, why would I make my title song on my first album a rock track?

I always liked the hard stuff. Rap to me was a form of rock. When you listen to hip-hop, we never say, "We're gonna R&B the mic!" We say, "We're gonna *rock* the mic!" or "We're gonna *rock* the house."

To me rocking is just aggression. If you go along with everything, if you sing what everyone wants to hear, you're doing what's popular. You're pop. But if you say, "Fuck that. I don't understand why—I want to go against the grain." Then it's rock.

Even when I was doing pure hip-hop, I was always laying in guitar licks, just to add to the energy. I didn't invent that sound. Thanks to Rick Rubin, acts like the Beastie Boys, Run-DMC, and LL Cool J were all using rock hooks. And I loved the edge and power that some loud electric guitar chords brought to the mix. To me it made perfect sense. It made the rap harder.

By the time I got to my third album, *O.G.,* when I'd go into the studio in L.A., it felt like half the city knew Ice-T's every move. There'd be a gang of folks dropping by my studio sessions night and day. Vic came home—still on parole—and I immediately hooked him up as the drummer in the band. So we're recording *O.G.* and one night I had a whole band sitting in the room. I was working in the Sound Castle studio in Hollywood, and Ernie C. and Beatmaster V were pressuring me to let them play on the record.

"Why don't we just make a band?" I said. "We'll play gigs around L.A. just for the hell of it."

The rest of that original lineup was Mooseman on bass and D-Roc on rhythm guitar. We didn't do some big audition or citywide search. It was just the dudes I'd been tight with for years. Moose went to Crenshaw with us and was a *beast* on the bass. D-Roc was one of Ernie's students. So now we had enough people for a band to start doing local gigs. This was in 1990.

We would play anywhere there were "open band" nights. We played little bars and pizza joints, not making any money, just testing out the Body Count concept. Then the cats from Dirty Rotten Imbeciles, one of the earliest hardcore thrash bands, were going out and they had some spot gigs in Northern California. They asked us if we want to go out with them and put ourselves in front of a real audience.

So we headed up to Northern Cali, did these gigs with DRI. There were skinheads with tattoos in the audience and they were booing us, wondering what a bunch of black street dudes were doing gigging at a thrash-punk show. Five minutes into the set they'd flipped and they were slamdancing. They were *gone.*

We didn't even know if we would be accepted by rock audiences. We didn't have some big strategic plan. I mean, Body Count was a garage band in every sense of the word. We just wanted to jam together and have fun. I never thought I could get a record deal where I could be the front man in the band. Since I was already signed to Sire for a few more albums, I didn't think we could get a separate deal.

But I said, "Fuck it, let's figure it out when it happens."

We did our first tour and went out with the groups DRI and Exodus. And we did a tour up and down the coast. We were just slamming it. The rock guys were digging us. More important, we had a really good time out there.

We were steadily gigging. We developed a tighter set. We realized we needed more songs—our set was too short. Ernie hooked us up with Perry Farrell from Jane's Addiction. Perry pitched me this idea of doing a cover of the Sly Stone song "Nigger/Whitey" for this video they were doing called *Gift.* I was going to do it as Ice-T instead of as a character. We were playing our parts. "I'm going to sing it at you, then you sing it at me," Perry told me, "I don't like you, you don't like me." I liked the concept of the remake.

"Don't call me 'nigger,' whitey!"

"Don't call me 'whitey,' nigger!"

We did the track and Perry started telling us about this idea he had to start up a traveling festival called Lollapalooza, kind of a Woodstock for heavy metal, alternative, punk, and hip-hop acts.

It sounded way too crazy to me—but I like shit that sounds way too crazy. Without hesitation I told Perry, "Look man, I want to be down. Put Ice-T on the bill." I don't think Perry even knew I had a rock band called Body Count.

There wasn't any expectation for that Lollapalooza show. They told me where to show up, when I was playing on the bill.

"Ice, you're going to go on third. It's going to be Butthole Surfers, then Rollins Band, then you."

"Shit," I said. "I go on after two established artists?"

"You're a platinum artist, Ice."

They told me I had an hour on the stage. An Ice-T set is normally an hour, but I decided I'd split it right down the middle, do thirty minutes of Ice-T material, thirty minutes of Body Count. They didn't pay me enough to bring all the guys in the band out, but I figured, *Fuck it, this is our chance.* I ate any profit from the show by bringing all the band and equipment out—twice as many people as normal—on the road.

After I did my Ice-T set, I paused and looked out at about twenty-thousand people.

"Now I'm about to prove to you that rock-n-roll has nothing to do with black and white," I said. "Rock-n-roll is a *state of mind.* . . ."

While I'm saying that our roadies have transformed the set to the Body Count stage, and then Ernie C. and D-Roc came in hard on the guitars. Boom. We hit them with "Cop Killer," "KKK Bitch," "Voodoo." And we *killed* it. All the hard shit had everybody's jaws dropping open. We'd play and Henry Rollins would stand on the side of the stage every night. We just went out there with a fever and nailed it.

I didn't have any fear. I looked at Ernie, Vic, Moose, and D-Roc back-stage. Every one of us looked like we'd just run a marathon. We were out of breath; all drenched in sweat. But the cats in the band all looked like they'd had the best time of their lives.

"Look," I told them. "We can do this. I can scream just as hard as any of these muthafuckas. And you guys can fucking *play.*"

Living Colour was also on the bill, but I saw our bands as polar opposites. Living Colour was the "black" band and we were the "niggers." Vernon Reid still adopted the rock look, bright colors, tight pants, a rock vibe. We had on khakis and looked like gangbangers. We had a style similar to Suicidal Tendencies; Mike Muir and those cats took that Venice gangster image and ran with it. We give credit to those guys in Suicidal as being the first gangster-based rock band. With Body Count, I wanted to have a Black Sabbath sound and style but my lyrics would be based on our lives. Ozzy and Dio would sing about the Devil; if you look at our debut album cover, when you open it, there's a guy with a gun pointed at your face. To us *that* was the devil. We wanted to change the imagery of metal to reality, like what's more scary than that: some gangster with a gat pointed at you?

The cover was supposed to be a super-gangbanger, some arch-criminal of the street—maybe based on a guy like Tookie, with COP KILLER tattooed on his chest. That guy on the cover didn't look like he had a friend in the world; he was dangerous, the last motherfucker you'd want to meet on the street. In other words, he was the gatekeeper of Hell. That was more reality-based for us than the standard heavy-metal artwork of Lucifer with horns and a pitchfork.

WE WANTED THE NAME Body Count to have a couple of meanings. It meant: How many people would die in the pit? How many other bands would we have to take out? How many nonbelievers could we turn into fans? Between us, we often called the group B.C. which was a play on words, too—that stood for Bloods and Crips. On our third album, *Violent Demise,* we even used the hand signs of the Bloods and the Crips, side by side, as the cover art.

Of course, any time you do anything new, people got shit to say. What the fuck is Ice doing? Is he posing? What's he trying to prove with this rock trip?

We got way more static from the white rock boys who didn't necessarily believe that we were serious. And I could understand that: Whenever you're deep with a whole culture, there is a fear of someone coming from outside, doing it just to make fun of it. When Eminem came into the rap game, we wanted to make sure that he really understood and had respect for the art of hip-hop. When Body Count hit the scene, the white rock crowd didn't know if it was just a gimmick, if my band was just studio players, and if we could actually play live.

But once people stood in front of us at a show and felt the *blast* of Body Count, damn straight, that doubt was soon removed. After our first few shows, most of the naysayers were silenced.

Then again, as an artist, you need the naysayers and the nonbelievers to add fuel to your creative fire. In a sense, that negativity is something that drives you.

After me, there was a big trend toward combining rock and hip-hop, with artists from Kid Rock to Limp Biskit expanding it to an entire genre. Earlier, Red Hot Chili Peppers was doing it. Anthony Kiedis was rapping. And the combination always worked; but if it doesn't have the tag "rap-rock," people don't realize it. I don't place Body Count in that category. I didn't want to do a rap-rock hybrid. Body Count was deliberately intended not to be hip-hop. I did not rap any of the lyrics. I already had an established rap identity. So the demarcation line between Ice-T and Body Count was very important to me. The album had to be straight-up rock. I wanted to tour with Slayer. I wanted to go out with Rollins Band. I wanted to hold my own with the real rock cats.

We did that first tour and then we didn't know what we were going to do with the band. Over at my label, Howie Klein got wind that I had a rock band. Seymour Stein was Howie's boss at Sire, but Howie was more the day-to-day guy, the guy in the trenches. So Howie Klein called me up and said, "Ice, I'll sign Body Count." I didn't even know that was possible, that I could have two separate deals at the same label, one for my hip-hop records and one for my metal band.

"Cool," I said, "Let's do this."

We went into the studio, laid down the tracks for our first self-titled album. The record contained the song "Cop Killer," and the cover art was that badass guy with the words *Cop Killer* tattooed on his chest. Everybody at Warner Bros. was happy with the album. Nobody had a problem with *shit*. Life was nearly perfect.

But, we'd later see a different side of everything—and everybody.

ON THE STRENGTH of that first record we hit the road. Pretty fast, Body Count picked up a following, especially internationally. Soon we were jetting all over the world. By 1993, we were touring Europe, even hitting Australia, New Zealand, and Japan.

It was during our first gig in Italy that some real craziness popped. The thing about playing a rock gig in Italy—which I didn't know at the time—was some of the fans were a bit behind the curve. Back in the day, the old punk bands like the Sex Pistols and the Clash used to tour Europe, and the Italian punks, just like the English punks, used to spit on them. Freaky as that sounds, unloading a big gob of spit on your heroes was a sign of respect. Punk turned everything upside down that way. That was back in the mid-seventies, before AIDS, before everyone was freaked out about bodily fluids. These punks in Italy never got the memo that spitting was played out, and when we opened up our Italian tour these cats in the Milan arena were still on that trip.

In the middle of the stage, I grabbed the microphone and laid it down.

"Dig," I said. "You can go ape shit, you can jump on the stage and wild out—I don't give a fuck! But one rule: Don't fucking spit!" Most places they understood it, but maybe the Italians didn't understand my English. We soon found there were a few of these cats—soccer-hooligan-looking dudes—who were still into that spitting game.

We're into our first song and these dudes in the front row are spitting at us. Now I'm getting offended. Because number one: I'm not the Dead Kennedys or Jello Biafra. And number two: This ain't no 1977. Dog, spitting is fucking nasty—I don't know what kind of diseases you got in your fucking mouth.

Actually, the spit hadn't touched me yet. But from the first song, this one group of fans is steady spitting on Ernie. He's playing guitar right near the edge of the stage and there's this actual waterfall of saliva going over in his direction.

A few songs later, as we're getting ready to go into "Cop Killer," I walk over to Ernie. His guitar is drenched in spit. Ernie says, "It's mostly that one motherfucker in black right there."

I see this kid in a black T-shirt, stringy black hair. They're not even punk rockers, just some young asshole Italian kids. I looked at the kid in the black. He responds by spitting right on me.

Okay, cool, I got this.

At that moment, I forgot I was Ice-T, forgot I was onstage, forgot every goddamn thing. I just had to fuck this kid up. I went out to the edge of the stage. The stage didn't have a pit, it just had a gate, and I was able to get right out there to the edge above the kid in the black T-shirt.

"Yo!" I shouted. "Everybody put your hands in the air!"

And when they all put their hands in the air, I just leaned over and clocked the dude in his fucking nose. And I hit him hard! So hard he fell back into the audience. I was pissed off, pumped full of adrenaline and I just crashed him. I clocked him, and he fell back and I yelled "Cop Killer!" And then Ernie and the rest of the band launched into "Cop Killer."

The kid I hit was still down on the ground, but as I turned, a couple of his friends grabbed my arm and tried to pull me down into the crowd. One Italian kid tried to sock me, so now I'm fighting with about four or five of them. They're on the other side of the gate, and we're fighting over the edge of the gate. I've got tunnel vision: All I see is the mic stand. I grabbed it and started swinging, beating down mother-fuckers.

I'm cracking motherfuckers left and right. It was crazy, the song was halfway finished—I'm not singing, just swinging like a madman. The Italian crowd was getting heated, and I'm yelling "Yo! Yo! Yo!" hoping to keep things calm.

But then the crowd started to sing their soccer chants. Hundreds of them in unison doing these straight-up *we're-gonna-kill-you* chants.

We had to break the fuck out—mid-song.

The band threw down their instruments. I dropped the microphone stand. We all ran backstage. The promoter had to shut the concert down immediately. Lights up. Security shoved the whole crowd outside.

We stayed in the dressing room for a long time, trying to wait out the mayhem, but the mob wasn't calming down. If anything they were getting more heated.

The whole band sat backstage, not sure what to do. The venue had only one exit—right out the front. The back of the arena led to a cliff, so there was no other way out. We sat there, sweating, glancing at one another. After about thirty minutes, I sent one of our roadies to do recon. He came back looking even more scared.

"Ice, the tour bus is fucked up. I don't know how we getting out of here." They fucked up our tour bus, rocking it back and forth, slashing the tires, smashing the windows.

"There still a lot of people outside?"

"About two hundred."

"Are they mad?"

"They're not waiting on autographs."

We sat there, trying to figure some way out, listening to the mob chanting. D-Roc had this brilliant plan to get us out the back of the venue, but because of the cliff, we ended up doing this long walk along the back of the venue, doubling right back to where we started. We didn't do fuck-all except walk a big perilous circle.

Then I told the promoter to call us about six cabs, and when they showed up, I said, "Okay, please—can we get the fuck out of here?"

"We'll run out fast—heads down," the promoter said. "Ice-T, you go last."

"Fuck that," I said, "I'm going first. They want my fuckin' head. They're after *me*."

We looked out front. Off to one side of the building, the crowd had started a big bonfire, so we didn't have much room to navigate. We knew they were going to shower us with bottles, rocks, bricks, anything they could hit us with. I started flashing back to my Rangers training.

"Yo," I said, "we gotta handle this like an ambush. They're trying to funnel us into the kill zone. That means the only thing we can do is attack the strongest position."

Sean E. Sean, Beatmaster V, D-Roc, the Italian promoter—they were all staring at me like I was insane.

"No, listen. This is the only way. We're going to run straight into the hurricane. If we get past the strong shit, we'll be safe."

We made our first direct assault. It was me, Sean E. Sean, Ernie, and the promoter. We dashed straight into the mob, and this brick came flying at us. Missed me by about five feet. Bottles are smashing; they're all screaming, but we somehow made it to the cab, with mobs of pissed-off Italians in hot pursuit. We piled into the taxi, but the cabdriver was so freaked out, he jumped out and ran away!

The mob surrounded the cab, but now we had no driver. The promoter was in the passenger seat, me, Ernie, and Sean E. Sean were in the back. The promoter was too scared to take the wheel, but I reached forward and smacked him in the head two times.

"Drive the car, muthafucka!"

The promoter slid over to the wheel. "But where—?"

"Just floor it!" I said.

So we stole that cab. Drove straight into the crowd. People were slamming their hands on the windows, dudes were bouncing off the hood. We didn't have a plan, just bashed our way out of the danger zone.

We wound through the dark streets of Milan, until we were about a mile away from the venue. Then I realized that in addition to possible assault and inciting a riot charges, we were not doing ourselves any favors by driving around in a stolen taxicab. We jumped out in the middle of the street. I ordered the promoter to take the cab back to the venue before we found ourselves looking at grand theft auto—or whatever was the Italian legal equivalent.

We walked along these medieval Italian streets, almost deserted now. It's pitch-black outside, and we were all wearing our black Body Count coats. Suddenly, I realized that we must look like one of the marauding gangs in *The Warriors*.

"Oh shit! We've got our colors on. Take them shits off, man! The whole city's fucking after us!"

We flagged down another cab, and as soon as we got in, the idiot smiled from ear to ear.

"Oh! You Americans? Let me take you to this very cool concert happening right now. Ice-T!"

He tried to pull a U-turn to take us back to the venue until we started screaming for him to drive us to the fucking hotel.

We made it back to the hotel and bunkered down for the night. All night the Italian radio and TV kept blaring a news flash: "Rapper Ice-T beats his fans up!"

After a few hours without any sleep, we slipped out of the hotel. We had to catch a train to Rome. We walked through the city all huddled up, wearing ball caps and hoodies, and got on the train. A few hours later we finally arrived in Rome, went straight from the train station to meet up with the country's number one rock DJ. We were told he was the most popular and most influential radio personality in Italy.

In the few hours of our traveling, the media had blown the episode up even further. The press was making it like I was disrespecting all of Italy.

We went into the studio. The DJ and I shook hands and he went right on the air live. Talking lightning-fast in Italian. All I could catch were a few syllables . . . "Ice-T" . . . "Body Count" . . . "Milano . . ."

Then he flipped into English and asked me what happened.

"Man, we were having a great show. Then guys in the front row were spitting on us. I asked them several times to stop spitting on us. Long story short, I ended up punching a guy in the face."

I didn't know how this DJ was going to react. But he flipped the script. I later found out what he told his audience in that staccato Italian:

Look, Italy, we love Ice-T. What did we expect him to do? This is why we love Ice-T. 'Cause he's a gangster. Because if you disrespect him, yes, he will punch you in the face!

Some clowns tried to ruin his concert. We should be angry at them. Ice-T is a guest in our country, we invited him to do all these sold-out shows, and we love him!

So he flipped the whole shit on the assholes who'd been spitting. We'd escaped the Milan mayhem and we needed him to squash the situation for the next shows we had to do. There was a real risk the rest of our European tour would go up in smoke. But due to him being the man, he was able to flip it 180 degrees. Instead of the line playing in the media that Ice-T had disrespected Italy, he made it clear that a handful of idiots had disrespected Ice-T.

We drove through the narrow Roman streets, winding over to the next arena. Sound check was no drama, and all the cats at the venue were shaking their heads, saying they were embarrassed by the behavior of those fans in Milan.

One thing I learned about Italians. They're hot-blooded. Proud as hell. Easy to rile up. But they also respect the fact that you'll stand up for yourself. By the rest of the shows in Italy, the whole story had reversed and all the Italians I met told me, "Look, Ice, we apologize for Milan."

We loved the rest of our European gigs. Of course—it goes without saying—we haven't been back to Milan since!

11.

WHEN I WROTE "Cop Killer," I thought it was just another rock song. Call me naïve, but I believed, as an artist, that every subject was fair game. I'm one of those people who thought that when they said "America is the land of free speech," they were sincere. I thought free speech meant I could say whatever I wanted to say.

So I just spit it out. I didn't give it too much afterthought.

The record had been out for a whole year; it was on Body Count's debut album. But we'd performed "Cop Killer" a full year before that on the Lollapalooza Tour. That made the song—if not the record—about two years old. The album came out, was selling well, and all of a sudden this organization called CLEAT (Combined Law Enforcement Associations of Texas) started calling for people to boycott Time Warner and get "Cop Killer" removed from stores. Other police groups soon joined them, railing about the record.

I'll never forget the moment. I was at home playing a video game called Tecmo-Bowl with four of my boys when Sean E. Sean called me.

"Yo! Check the TV! The President is on the news, talking about 'Cop Killer.'"

We flipped the channel to CNN and it wasn't President Bush, actually. It was Vice President Dan Quayle, talking about me, looking *pissed,* saying the name "Ice-T" like he had shit on his tongue, calling my record "obscene."

As soon as Quayle said, "Ice-T," there was a collective groan around my living room.

Ah shit.

I knew the band and I were in for some drama.

But at first, it just seemed stupid to me. Petty and ridiculous. Why were they tripping? First off, it wasn't like "Cop Killer" was a novel concept. There'd already been a group called Millions of Dead Cops. There'd been a movie out called *Cop Killer,* a book called *Cop Killer,* and Black Flag had been doing superaggressive songs like this long before Body Count.

I thought I was in a fairly safe zone of self-expression. I thought—especially within the world of rock and roll—that I was free to write what I wanted. I was actually listening to one of Seymour Stein's favorite rock bands, the Talking Heads, and had their song "Psycho Killer" on my mind and one day I just said, "Fuck it, I'll make a song called 'Cop Killer.'" I wanted to blend the sound of speed metal with a topic that was real to Body Count's lives.

As the controversy continued to build, our jaws stayed dropped. I kept saying, "What the fuck? It's a song. It's an *old* song. It's a protest record. It's a song about a guy who lost his mind over brutal cops."

I told a group of reporters: "I'm singing in the first person as a character who is fed up with police brutality. I ain't never killed no cop. I felt like it a lot of times. But I never did it. If you believe that I'm a cop killer, you believe David Bowie is an astronaut."

It was an election year, and the political powers started to use "Cop Killer" in this nationwide campaign for "family values" and against violent lyrics in rap music. That in itself was bogus because it was a rock record, a Body Count song, and had nothing to do with gangsta rap. Second, the lyrics were coming out of the head of the character I'd created. It was a scenario. It wasn't my personal view. I wasn't calling on cops to be killed. The character was saying, "Fuck police brutality. Cops have been brutal to me, so tonight I'm going to kill some."

But at the time, cops were under siege. This is pre–Rodney King— before the acquittal of the officers who had been caught on tape severely beating a black motorist, but not too long before—and there was a lot of media attention on the subject of police brutality. And because it was a Presidential election year somebody thought this was a good issue to exploit politically. It made great fodder for the Republican stump speeches. Let's attack Warner Bros. Because after the initial criticism broke, the hostility wasn't directed so much at me. A greater anger was directed at Time Warner for allowing the song to be put out. Ice-T— they could write me off as just another pissed-off black man from the 'hood. But Time Warner? You're a Fortune 500 company. You've got a big gleaming office tower in midtown Manhattan. You're supposed to be one of *us.* You're supposed to part of the system—why are you putting this "Cop Killer" shit on the market?

We all kept thinking it would go away.

But it kept getting bigger and bigger and bigger. Then Charlton Heston and the NRA got involved. President Bush publicly denounced Time Warner and any company that would release a record like "Cop Killer." The former president of the National Association of Chiefs of Police, Dennis Martin, actually—and ludicrously—claimed that the song had encouraged violence against police: "The 'Cop Killer' song has been implicated in at least two shooting incidents and has inflamed racial tensions in cities across the country. . . . It is an affront to the officers—one hundred forty-four in 1992 alone—who have been killed in the line of duty while upholding the laws of our society and protecting all its citizens."

At a campaign fundraising luncheon, Dan Quayle kept ratcheting up his rhetoric. "I am outraged at the fact that Time Warner, a major corporation, is making money off a record called 'Cop Killer' that suggests it is okay to kill cops."

It got to the point that people actually sent death threats to Warner Bros.—it was some real shit.

Now, looking back on it, this is what I learned: Yes, you have the right to say whatever you want in America, but you have to be prepared for the *ramifications* of what you say. When I yelled "Cop Killer," I did not prepare for the fallout. I'd been dissing rappers for years; they didn't do shit. Then I dissed the cops—and they came after me like no gang I've ever encountered. Then Charlton Heston, Tipper Gore, and the President of the United States himself came after me.

I TELL PEOPLE TODAY that you don't know what heat is until you've had the President of the United States say your name in anger. Because the minute he does—*boom*—the deepest security check of your life immediately goes into action. The FBI, the Secret Service, the IRS, everybody gets into the game. Because he's the President of the United States. The next question from the President to his chief of staff will be, "What do we know about this man?"

Soon as the President says your name they do a four-bureau check. They dig up every speck of dirt they can find. They had my military records, and I'm sure they knew about my criminal background. But I don't think they gave a damn that I'd been involved in all kinds of robberies and mayhem back in the day. The truth is, they were really trying to find out if I was some Black Panther–type of rabble-rouser, if I was the kind of person who's trying to start a real social revolution, trying to sound a call to arms like Huey P. Newton. Was the record meant to be me standing on a soapbox? Me telling the youth of America that they should literally go out and kill the cops?

These are some intelligent guys in the FBI and Secret Service: I'm sure that when they checked out "Cop Killer," they knew it was just a *song.* A point-of-view song—okay, a little more intense, but not too far removed from Talking Heads' "Psycho Killer."

But the investigation was done. It had to be done. That's not because Ice-T is anyone important, it's just a rule of fact: the President shouldn't be saying your fucking name in anger. If he's mad at you, his boys in the Secret Service, FBI, and National Security are going to find out who the fuck you are. That's just how they get down.

But here's what's funny. It wasn't like it was hard to find out shit about me. I'm an open book. At the end of the day, I said, "Yo, if I was really on some political platform, and this is what I wanted, well, then, fuck it, I'll take the political heat." But that wasn't what I was out to do.

And if they'd been able to find anything from my criminal past they could use, come on, they'd have had me in shackles on the nightly news. They would have locked me *under* the jail. But the only dirt they could find on me was shit that I'd already claimed. What are they going to do? Give a press conference with Dan Quayle or Charlton Heston: "This man Ice-T is an ex-criminal." Come on! Who the fuck doesn't know that?

Here's something I never admitted before: One of the reasons I got into the record business and came clean about all the dirt I did was because I knew that fame doesn't allow you to hide much. You better just 'fess up. Fame is a fierce spotlight, but it's also a way to clean out your closet. You have to remember that in early hip-hop, telling the truth about your criminal life was not in vogue. When I came out, dudes were still saying, "Oh, I learned to sing in church." You didn't come out and say, "Yo, I'm an ex-thief" Or, "I'm a hustler from the streets of South Central." That didn't sell records. *Now* it does. *Now* everyone claims to have been a shot caller, bank-robber, gunslinger, murderer. But that's really my blueprint.

It would have been a waste of time for me to pretend to be someone I'm not. So I chose to use it like Iceberg Slim did: as a source for my material.

When that national security search happens, you feel it from the other side—things like tax audits, covert surveillance; they even snatched my daughter out of school and asked her if I was a member of any paramilitary organizations! Funny part about it was, they never came to me directly. But I felt a certain level of scrutiny and surveillance twenty-four hours a day. Things you can't rationally explain are happening all around you. It's like you have an ice cream truck parked outside your house in the middle of the winter.

WHEN PEOPLE TALK TO ME about "Cop Killer" today, they often assume I'm bitter about the controversy. I only get angry when people overstep their boundaries. But with "Cop Killer" everybody at Time

Warner was doing what they thought was correct, at least from a business standpoint. People needed to do what they thought had to be done. Everybody was doing their job. I look at it this way: When a cop busts you for selling coke, don't get pissed at the cop. The law was there. You knew it, you broke it; the cop did his job. So how can you get mad? How can you hold a grudge?

To be real—even in the hottest days of that media frenzy—I felt bad for Time Warner. I felt awful for them. To me Time Warner wasn't some massive, faceless corporate entity. I had good personal relationships with Seymour Stein, Mo Ostin, Lenny Waronker—even the chief executive of Time Warner, Gerald Levin.

In fact, right before the shit hit the fan, I'd just been up at the Time Warner world headquarters in this massive boardroom, speaking to Gerald Levin and all the top-dog executives. That was a pretty big deal; they didn't have every artist on Warner Bros. up in their board meetings. They had guys like former president Nixon speak to them about economic and political issues. I was there with Quincy Jones, talking to the executives and board members, because we'd just won a Grammy Award for Best Rap Performance by a Duo or Group for "Back on the Block." We were their golden boys.

When the "Cop Killer" storm hit, the Time Warner executives understood the stakes.

"Ice, this is a bad day," Seymour Stein told me, "because once we allow them to tell us what we can and can't do, what we can and can't release, this whole division of music is pretty much through."

Warner Bros. was the home of the edgiest artists of the time: Prince, Madonna, Slayer, Sam Kinnison, Andrew Dice Clay, the Geto Boys, and me. Almost everybody considered raw and edgy signed to a major at the time was under the Warner Bros. umbrella.

People often make the mistake of thinking that Time Warner put pressure on me. They never put an ounce of pressure on me. I made the move on my own. When we were kids, if you were my buddy and I threw a rock and busted a school window and we both got in trouble— I'm going to tell them it was just me. I'm going to take that weight. You had nothing to do with the shit.

Same with "Cop Killer," I decided. *I wrote the song. I'll take the weight.*

I said to Warner Bros., "Know what? All I got in life is my integrity. If you want, we can pull the song off the album."

Critics were already saying I did the song for the money. Just to be scandalous. But I didn't give a fuck. The Body Count album was going to sell without that song on it. So Warner re-pressed the record, sold the Body Count album, and gave the "Cop Killer" single away for free.

But even with that concession, the climate just got too intense. It wasn't so much the political pressure as the financial stakes. When this shit happened, when Charlton Heston went into that shareholders meeting, thirty million dollars went into the balance. Charlton Heston, as the head of the National Rifle Association, impacted the Warner Bros. bottom line. He stood there in the meeting reading my lyrics like it was a page from the *Planet of the Apes* script.

I GOT MY 12 GAUGE SAWED OFF
I GOT MY HEADLIGHTS TURNED OFF
I'M ABOUT TO BUST SOME SHOTS OFF
I'M ABOUT TO DUST SOME COPS OFF . . .

He didn't even know what he was talking about. "These are the lyrics to 'Killer Cop,'" he said. "Oops, I mean 'Cop Killer.'" He's so outraged, yet he doesn't even know the name of the record? It was some crazy, hypocritical bullshit.

Charlton Heston railing at that meeting sent the Time Warner stock into a tailspin. In life, forget principles, forget egos—most people are all about money. Time Warner realized it was costing them big money to keep me around. They brought in a crisis specialist to look at my next set of recordings. I already had the *Home Invasion* album in the can, and I knew that some of the lyrics were going to raise eyebrows.

Don't give a fuck about a cop or a G-man
They all talk shit, breath smellin' like semen
I take 'em in the alley all alone
Put 'em in the prone
Pop-pop-pop to the dome.

So yes—I was still killing cops in my music.

And no—that wasn't going to make me any more popular at the label.

"Dig," I said, "All right, fine. Just give me a release from my contract. No harm no foul."

I still owed Warner two albums. I know Seymour Stein and Mo Ostin felt bad letting me out of my contract. But they understood I had to do what I had to do. I knew that if they put out any more Body Count or Ice-T albums, shit was going to be too hectic.

The reality to me was this: I knew they wouldn't promote the record anyway. Even if they released it, they would try to let it slip quietly under the radar. So I took my album over to Bryan Turner at Priority Records. And that was the end of my Warner Bros. adventure.

A lot of folks get it twisted, but this is the deal: Time Warner was just looking out for itself. And I respected that. I still respect that. They never treated me like shit, never got mad or yelled at me. All those theories you still hear today—Time Warner sold Ice down the river— hell naw. They didn't! It was just a *gang* of political and financial pressure.

People think controversy helps your bottom line, but I disagree. There is a big tradeoff: Yes, you sell some records, but with all the static—the cancellation of concerts, the hike in insurance for the shows you do get—there are way more costs that come along with controversy than benefits. I would never advise people that controversy is the way to blow up. You'll become *known* but will it translate into money? Probably not.

I always felt like I was the cat who was on the firing line. I was out there on that thin horizon, right at the edge of shit. If you fast-forward a few years, Ted Turner pushed Death Row Records off Interscope over similar issues. It was a trickle-down effect. And because of that trickle-down, I caught a lot of flack from different rap groups: *Ice-T, you caved. You gave in to the Man.* Side-bettors were out there, throwing in their opinions, trying to hurt my name. It's funny that the rap community ended up coming down on me harder than anyone in the mainstream. *The Source* magazine went in on me. Over and over. An editor at *The Source,* Reginald Dennis, came at me with one particularly hard editorial: "When he voluntarily removed 'Cop Killer' from the *Body Count* album," he wrote, "Ice-T allowed a devastating precedent to be set, opening the door for widespread censorship of rap."

As far as the hip-hop world was concerned, I went from being a guy who was standing up for freedom of expression to being some weak-kneed motherfucker who wouldn't speak truth to power.

But to me, the key to winning the game is: Don't worry about *everyone*. Find out who's really on your team and then roll with them.

My man Chuck D put it best. "If you ain't in the battles," Chuck said, "you shouldn't comment on the war."

Chuck knew what I was dealing with. He'd had his own media battles with Public Enemy. So I always had the dudes I respected in hip-hop, cats like Chuck, telling the haters and side-bettors to shut the fuck up.

Walk in my shoes for a day. That was some stressful, hectic shit. That was heat coming from the *government* of the United States. I was in quicksand for months. There was no safe ground to stand on.

PART FIVE

NINETY-NINE PROBLEMS

"THE MOST DANGEROUS THING ON EARTH ISN'T A GUN, KNIFE OR BOMB. IT'S EGO."

—ICE-T'S DAILY GAME

12.

MY CAREER AS A TELEVISION ACTOR all started with Fab 5 Freddy. In addition to being a hip-hop "personality," the host of *Yo! MTV Raps,* Fab's also a respected visual artist—Fred Brathwaite—and he used to show his work in some of the swanky L.A. galleries where Darlene worked for a while. We have been friends forever. We're pimp buddies—we sit back and talk a lot of fantastic shit!

Fred was chilling at my house. At that time I had a couple of screen credits; I'd done *New Jack City,* I'd done *Trespass.* We were just chopping it up when Andre Harrell called. Freddy put me on the phone and Andre, who'd branched from his music executive career into TV production, asked me to do *New York Undercover,* a drama starring Malik Yoba and Michael DeLorenzo as police detectives.

Andre was getting at me about coming on the show. I was playing it cold.

"Man, listen, I'm in the *movies.* I don't do that TV shit."

"Come on, Ice."

"Plus, let me tell you. Y'all ripped off *New Jack City*!"

"Oh, you're too big now, huh?" Andre said. He pulled that "black solidarity" card on me. "You can't help out a brother, huh?"

I said, "Okay, give me a bad-guy character and I'll play it."

The character was named Danny Up, some eccentric kind of criminal who was supposed to be running an early meth lab.

It sounded pretty out there so I said, "Cool."

I FLEW TO NEW YORK to do the show, and it was a great experience. It was shot just like a movie. They respected the shit out of me, and I had a great time.

It was a one-off, but at the end of my shoot, they got the dailies, liked what they saw, and I got another call.

"Ice, would you stay around? We don't want to kill you at the end of the episode."

I told them no way.

When you do television, there's a salary cap for guest stars. Back then it was only about $7,000. Networks and production companies do that so that guest stars have no leverage to negotiate. If I did a guest spot on *New York Undercover,* I got the same money as Henry Winkler. Seven grand wasn't really cutting it for me. After taxes and expenses—I had to put Sean E. Sean up in a hotel—and partying in New York, I walked away with a grand.

They asked me to stay but I said, "Naw, I gotta get back to L.A."

The producers said, "We can't pay you more, but we can sweeten the deal. We can get you more perks, put you in a better hotel." They put us in a better hotel and covered Sean's bills.

So I said, "Fuck it," and I ended up doing two more shows. I got to be in the cliffhanger—the season's final episode—and I got to kill Malik Yoba's baby. I was cutting fingers off. I was a beast. Doing some crazy-ass sinister shit—I had a great time!

Dick Wolf was the executive producer of *New York Undercover,* but I didn't know anything about him. Honestly, I'd never watched an episode of *Law & Order.* After my experience on *New York Undercover,* the Dick Wolf "machine" knew my style—they liked me.

A few months later, I had an idea for this show called *Players,* which was a story about guys who go to prison and get turned around and come out and create a vigilante army. I decided I'd pitch the show directly to Dick Wolf, so I called his office up and said I want to have a meeting.

Dick Wolf is a big ominous character. To be honest, he looks more like an old-school mobster than a big television executive. He looks exactly like the guy that would be sitting at the head of the table in any big Mob organization.

By the time of our first meeting, of course, I'd learned Dick Wolf's history. Dick started off as a writer, he wrote for television back in the days of *Hill Street Blues* and *Miami Vice.* He knew his shit backward and forward.

I came into his office and pitched him my idea for *Players* and he just stared at me, with a real cold expression.

"Every *single* actor has an idea for his own show."

I'm a bit taken aback, but I don't try to argue; I'm still waiting for him to give me a bit of feedback.

"Kind of sounds like *The A-Team.*"

Shit. He thinks I'm biting Mr. T?

There's a long pause. I don't say anything. Finally, Dick Wolf says, "*A-Team* saved ABC."

I stood there nodding.

"Do you mind if I mess around with it?" he says.

"Naw, go ahead."

I leave the meeting. I ask my manager, Jorge, "What the fuck just happened in there?"

"I wish I could tell you," Jorge says. "Nobody really knows what Dick Wolf is thinking."

Weeks went by. No word. I assumed my idea was dead in the water. It was at least a month later that I got a phone call. It was Dick.

"Hey Ice-T, guess what?"

"What?"

"I'm sitting on a plane with Warren Littlefield." Warren was the head of NBC Universal at the time.

"That's cool," I said.

"You have a television show," Dick said.

Dick pitched the show to him as they sat right next to each other in first class, and he got the green light right there on the plane.

"Well, what does that mean?"

"It means we're good to go," he said. "We'll be getting back to you."

They got back at me. They had a writer named Reggie Rock Bythewood who used to be on staff at *New York Undercover*. They brought him in and twisted the show a little bit. They turned us into federal criminals out on work-release to help the cops. It was done as a pseudo-comedy, wasn't real heavy or dark or hardcore.

Now I had my own show. But like they say, "Be careful what you wish for." It's one thing to be a guest star, or even have a recurring role on network television like I'd experienced on *New York Undercover*. But if you're the *star* of one of these network dramas, there is no harder job in Hollywood: A lead actor will work fourteen hours a day, five days a week, shooting for eleven months out of the year.

One of the perks of the gig was that I had my own trailer on the Universal lot. I used to get up in the morning and the tram would be rolling by and I'd hear the P.A. booming: "This is Ice-T's trailer. He's shooting his show called *Players*."

I was usually running on fumes; four hours of sleep. The tram would roll past and make the announcement. I'd wipe the sleep out of my eyes and stare out the trailer window.

"Yo, I'm a stop on the tour."

We had a good run with *Players*. We lasted a year. If there's any reason it failed it was that it was on too early. Our slot had us up against *Sabrina the Teenage Witch* and Urkel from *Family Matters*. We did fine; after a few months, we knocked Urkel out. But NBC was really cocky back then. They had *Seinfeld* and *Friends*. They were the top dogs. Back then it was normal to get ratings numbers in the twenties—today, they're dying to get a four-share.

So NBC was real hardcore; if we wasn't winning our time slot—and at one point we made it up to number two—then we weren't getting renewed. At the end of the full twenty-three episodes, they canceled the show.

I'll never forget how I got the news. Dick Wolf called me personally and said, "I wish I had a stronger vehicle for you, Ice."

I'd learned a lot. I was a producer on *Players,* so I got to sit in on the production meetings, got to see the inner workings of TV. I began to realize how different movies and TV are. If you make a movie, it either hits or it flops. Television is like making a movie every week. You have all these competitors, ratings numbers coming in every week, it can be nerve-racking. There's only so much you can do. There are so many variables: Is the network spending enough on promotion? Is your picture on the side of every city bus? All you can do is just try to be the best actor you can be; the rest of it is really out of your hands.

One thing about Dick Wolf: he's never crossed me, never lied to me. If he makes a deal with you verbally, then that's the deal. You don't have to wait for a bunch of lawyers to draw up the contracts. We appreciate that straight-shooting style in each other. He once said, "Ice-T is the least-pain-in-my-ass."

Dick works from a pool of actors that he likes. Guys like Costas Mandylor and Frank Hughes had been on *Law & Order.* They came over and co-starred on *Players.* After the cancellation, Dick Wolf hired me for a new show he had called *Swift Justice*—then he called me back to do *Law & Order Exiles,* the full-length television film with Chris Noth making his comeback.

The good thing about the Wolf team is that if they like you, they'll return to that pool to hire from over and over.

I WAS STILL KNEE-DEEP in the fast-changing record business. I was running my own label, Coroner Records, and we were trying to be the first company to do hip-hop on the Internet. We'd inked a deal with Atomic Pop. My manager, Jorge, Sean E. Sean, and me were doing some Coroner Records business and for some reason we decided to go to Roscoe's. Now, understand, I never eat at Roscoe's House of Chicken and Waffles. Despite what most people think, not *every* black person in L.A. eats there. I like some chicken and waffles, but Roscoe's is not one of my hangouts.

Soon as we walk in the door, who's there eating chicken and waffles? Dick Wolf and his publicist.

I haven't seen Dick in a long time so we said what's up. How's it going. Then we left.

His publicist later told me that's where Dick got the idea to put me in his new show, *Law & Order: SVU.* "The show was struggling to get its footing, just out the gate, and Dick was trying to figure out what to do, and when he saw you, a light went off, and he said, 'Let's put Ice in the show.'"

That's how it's done. In this business, when people say, "Out of sight, out of mind," it's *real*—and a lot of times there's a million-dollar check hanging in the balance. Just having your face pop in front of a Hollywood heavyweight randomly at Roscoe's Chicken and Waffles can break your career open in a new direction.

Now when I got the call to come do *Special Victims Unit,* believe it or not, I really didn't want to do it.

I was sitting on the fence with the scripts for a long time. It wasn't that I didn't want to do *Law & Order,* but I wasn't sure I was ready to move to New York. Secondly, I'd come off *Players* and I was a star. And like I said, that's a brutal work schedule, fourteen hours a day, five days a week—you have no life.

I'd rather have less money and more freedom.

But they kept reassuring me. "This is an ensemble cast. You don't work all the days. Just come do four shows, Ice."

"Okay, that sounds cool."

I agreed to do four shows.

I've stayed eleven years.

STAY ON THIS EARTH long enough and life will definitely come and bite you in the ass.

In was a beautiful afternoon in April 1999, and I was sitting in my office in Hollywood, feeling like I was on top of my game. Feeling like things could not get any smoother.

By the mid-nineties, after all that heat for "Cop Killer" and my struggles with Time Warner, I was running my label, Coroner Records, the way I wanted to run it. We'd hooked the office up: black sofas, black rugs, framed gold and platinum records. Even a replica on the ceiling of Michelangelo's rendering of Adam's outstretched finger touching the hand of God. I always loved beginning my day staring up at that image of the birth of man from the Sistine Chapel.

In spring of '99, I found myself at a major transition: Up till this point, I had made my name as a gangsta rapper. The godfather of the West Coast hip-hop scene. I'd made a lot of waves, and sold a lot of records, both as a solo artist and with Body Count.

My day-to-day was primarily as a music exec. I was putting in long days running Coroner Records from my ninth-floor office on Hollywood Boulevard. Behind the scenes, I was constantly bringing my old criminal partners out of the street life, showing them that there was a legal way to make money. I had Sean E. Sean working as my right-hand man. I was known as being one dude from the streets who didn't forget his homeboys. Between bail and legal fees, I literally spent millions of dollars helping friends of mine get back on the street.

I was about to go to New York to start shooting my first season of *Law & Order: SVU*. I had a pile of *SVU* scripts that Dick Wolf had sent sitting on my big oak desk.

I was rereading one of the *SVU* scripts, trying to visualize how I was going to portray Detective Odafin "Fin" Tutuola, when around one PM I got word that one of my old partners was coming up to the label.

His name was Deon, but on the streets of South Central everyone called him Baby D. He was about ten years younger than me and, when I was hustling, he became one of my crime partners. I put him in the game. We did a lot of licks together. He got locked up for a gun charge, and while he was in the pen, I looked out for his family. When he came back home, I told him he could work for me. I even gave him a rap group to manage.

Baby D was what we called a *transformer*, a cat who dresses like a square by day—straight-up business attire, like he's got a manager's job at Office Depot or owns his own towing company—but in reality, he's an O.G. Crip.

So on this particular April afternoon, Baby D comes up to the label. And while we're kicking it, he casually shows me his gun: a semiautomatic, two-tone pistol, brushed aluminum with a black slide. He asked me if we had any guns up in the office. "No, we ain't got no heat up in here," I said. "A lot of my friends are on parole and they can't be around no weapons." I didn't think much more of it at the time.

Baby D split, and five hours later, we were just chilling out in the office, about ready to head home for the day. It was DJ Evil E, Sean E. Sean, my man Rich, my daughter, LeTesha—then twenty-three years old—and one of her girlfriends. Suddenly, we saw on the closed circuit monitors that three guys had come into the lobby unannounced. They looked like rappers. We used to have rappers rolling through all the time, looking to get signed. I sent my boy Rich to the front door to let them in.

A few minutes passed. Rich hadn't returned. Next thing, these two cats bust through the door with their Roscoes out. I thought it was some of my people playing around, because I got friends who'll mess with you like that. But these were some serious dudes. For a second, I thought I might get the jump on them, but then I realized that the third guy had my boy Rich on the ground with a pistol to his head. So if there's any kind of struggle or commotion in my office, they'll definitely rock Rich.

We underwent what I call the jacker's protocol. When dudes come through the door with guns, I understand the psychology only too well—I know how they're going to get down, because I've been on the other side of the gun. They're either coming to kill you or they're not. They're not going to decide halfway through—on the spur of the moment—that they're going to execute five, six, seven people.

The deal is this: If they come through the door with masks on, they're probably *not* going to kill you. If they don't have masks on, more than likely you're going to die. These cats didn't have masks on. But for some reason, I didn't think they had it in them to murder us.

It was precision work. I almost had to admire their efficiency. They lined us all up, screaming orders.

"Yo, run that muthafuckin' watch! Run that muthafuckin' chain!"

They snatched my Rolex Presidential, my gold medallion, and my ring that everyone called "the power source"—a huge, flawless diamond piece that was worth about seventy thousand dollars.

They ordered us all into the kitchen, and then I saw one of them wiping the fingerprints off the doorknobs with his shirt. My thoughts were racing.

For a second, I saw all these TV stations breaking in with the news that Ice-T had joined the ranks of Biggie and Tupac—another rap icon murdered by unknown gunmen.

But I snapped out of it and focused on the here-and-now.

Okay, what's their next move? I was down on one knee, like a sprinter at the starting blocks, ready to lunge at one of them if they started busting shots.

And then my eyes focused on the little dude's gun. It was the same two-tone brushed aluminum pistol that Baby D had showed me earlier. They flicked off all the lights, and just when I thought they were going to start busting shots, they turned and ran. We could hear them in the lobby, laughing and yelling, "Yo, I can't believe we did it!"

THAT NIGHT I CALLED a meeting at my house in the hills. My place was swarming with fifty or sixty dudes. Heavy-hitting cats from all kinds of gang sets—dozens of O.G.'s and shot callers. It was like a massive gang summit: everybody showed up saying, "Ice, are you all right?" The news of the robbery had traveled like a brushfire around L.A. Everybody was perplexed. They kept saying, "Ice got so much love in the streets—who'd have the *balls* to do this shit?"

We started doing our detective work, and I told my people that one of the jackers had used a two-tone semiautomatic piece identical to Baby D's.

That was the coldest blow—when that realization sunk in. I didn't want to believe the facts at first. My mind was rationalizing it, playing tricks on me. I mean, who can protect themselves from betrayal? The day your brother wakes up and plans to do you dirty—there's no defense against that.

All my people were telling me, "Ice, just put the green light out on him—everybody knows Baby D crossed you. Cats are only giving him a pass because he's *your* friend."

I was even more pissed because my daughter had been in harm's way, but still I didn't want to order this dude killed.

After some "street therapy"—some calming words from my closest friends—I chilled down a bit. But the situation was still very volatile.

Three weeks later, we were in line outside the Palace Theater. We were five deep. I had four other guys with me. And I was also carrying a .380 Pocketlite. L.A. is not like New York; everybody carries guns. L.A. is the wild fucking West. There's heat always. It affects the way you move. You got to handle life like that. Any argument can turn into a shootout.

So we were at the club and I got my .380 in my front pocket. We were on high alert because memories of the robbery were still fresh in everyone's minds.

"Yo," one of my boys said, "dude is standing right behind us."

I turned. Baby D was about forty feet behind us with a girl.

The clown had the nerve to send the girl up to us in the line. "He said, 'Tell Ice I want to talk to him.'"

I nearly flipped. "What?" I said. "You tell that bitch-ass nigga if he got something to say to me to come up *here* and talk to me!"

It was a standoff. He thought I was about to walk back to him.

And, honestly, if he had walked up to me—me and all my boys being strapped—some unforgivable shit might have went down right there in front of the Palace Theater.

But he didn't move. And I didn't move. I told my friends, "Come on. Let's break the fuck out." We just had to pimp past it.

I probably saved Baby D's life right then and there. If I'd even given the nod to my boys, it would have gone down on some O.K. Corral–type shit.

A few days later, I confronted Baby D. I called him up from my office at Coroner Records.

"Yo, I'm not even angry at you, man," I said. "I'm just hurt. But I got bigger things to deal with right now."

"Naw, man. It wasn't me!" he said. "Niggas is spreading shit about me."

"I got bigger moves to make with my life."

Baby D never copped to it. He couldn't cop to it. But we all knew what he'd done.

The next morning, I jetted out to New York to start shooting my first season of *Law & Order: SVU*. While I was on location in Manhattan, I got the call from my boy Sean E. Sean back in L.A.

The streets had caught up to Baby D. He was found murdered with two shells in his dome. Rumor had it, he'd robbed some big-timers of their drug stash and these dudes didn't waste any time exacting their revenge.

I learned a lesson that day—a real jewel. Keep your eyes peeled for every sign of betrayal. I mean, there were little hints of disloyalty from Baby D that I ignored; truthfully, I didn't *want* to see them.

A lot of times in life you'll run into snakes and assholes, and you'll feel it's your job to straighten them out. But remember this: If a dude is a snake to you, odds are he's a snake to everybody. That's what we call his "get down." Eventually, he's going to cross the wrong person. You don't have to make it your job to be the hand of God.

13.

AFTER THE SETUP, I knew I had to close my circle. I had to tighten up the people I considered worthy of trust.

Right after that heavy situation with Baby D, everything in my life flipped. There was upheaval on every level: physical, professional, romantic. First off, I permanently relocated, from Los Angeles to New York. Second, I was starting a new job at NBC. And, though I didn't realize it right away, my relationship with Darlene was coming to an end.

IN NEW YORK, my life became all about work. I didn't have a lot of time to ruminate or feel bad about our relationship ending. I was losing myself in my new job. Working harder than ever as I leapt into my new role on *Law & Order: SVU*.

I'd always had a fondness for New York; I'd had a solid connection to the city ever since I linked up with Afrika Islam, Grandmaster Caz, Melle Mel, and the other New York hip-hop pioneers. Now I was not only moving to the Big Apple, I was heading into the cast of probably the definitive New York TV franchise of our time.

Right away, I fell in love with the show. There's *nothing* like shooting on location on the New York streets. People walk up to you in between takes, telling you whatever's on their minds. New Yorkers don't give a fuck. They're not starstruck. They'll tell you if they think you're the bomb. They'll tell you if they think you're wack. But mostly—overwhelmingly—we get mad love from New Yorkers when we're out on locations. The streets and buildings of Manhattan have such a presence—like another character actor on the show—both on the original *Law & Order* and *Special Victims Unit*.

I don't think I'd like my job on *SVU* as much if we didn't do so many location shoots. Acting in a closed room, at least for me, sometimes feels boring and corny. You want to go out in the streets and see the people wave and hear them holler at you. My debut season on *SVU,* we were out doing scenes in the middle of Madison Avenue at first daylight, before the rush-hour madness makes it impossible to shoot, and people were stopping on every corner to watch. We were closing down sections of Central Park, throwing our lines back and forth, standing over pretend corpses in the grass. That was a trip.

When I joined the show, they had this backstory written for my character, Detective Tutuola: Fin's parents were supposed to be Black Panthers. I was an officer who studied for a law degree but decided not to take the bar exam. I mulled all that over, trying to let it seep into my consciousness. But none of that shit was really helping me with the character. At the end of the day, we found another motivational hook. One of the producers took me aside.

"Ice," he said, "you don't really like the cops, right?"

"No, man. I don't."

"But you admit you need them, right?"

"Yeah."

"So that's your role on this show: Play the cop that we need."

When you see me running around chasing fools on *SVU,* that's exactly the mantra I keep in my head. *Play the cop we need.* Whenever I show up on set, it's like I'm a little kid making believe I'm the police.

There's really nothing more complicated to it than that. I'm no method actor; I never spent months riding around with real-live NYPD detectives to get inside their brains, to turn myself into a pretend version of them. Hell no. I'll break it down: Fin is just Ice-T pretending to be police. All my scenes, all my lines, are filtered through my own personal perspective.

And the producers and writers are very responsive to me. If they write a scene for me and I say, "Naw, that's not how I feel" or "I would never say that shit," depending on how essential the dialogue is, the writers may change it.

One reason *SVU* has become the most successful of the *Law & Order* shows is the fact that we're truly an ensemble cast. The chemistry between us is great; all the stars and co-stars have such clear identities. We're not cartoons, but we're neatly delineated. There's very little ambiguity to our roles. And in the world of weekly TV shows, audiences connect with that kind of clarity.

Mariska Hargitay's character, Liv Benson, is supposed to be the child of rape. That defines her mind-set and makes her supersensitive to the victims. Chris Meloni, as Elliot Stabler, is defined primarily by his children, so he cycles almost every case through the lens of being a father. Plus, he's got *major* anger issues. Richard Belzer as Munch thinks every-fucking-thing is a massive conspiracy; he's very well read and verbose. Plus, he's a world-class wiseass. And I'm the guy on the squad who was supposed to have previously been an undercover narc—I'm point-blank, grew up in the streets, and I don't give a fuck for niceties. If we grab some child molester, I'm likely to give him a smack in the face as we shove him in the Crown Vic. I'm soft for the little kid victims, but I'm not too subtle or sensitive when it comes to any of the sexual predators we've got to lock up.

Those are four very clear personality types; they set up four different points of view. When you put me together with Chris, you know that he's the rageaholic, but if he crosses some legal boundaries, I've got his back. When I'm working one-on-one with Mariska, she's going to get sensitive, but I'm more like the no-nonsense cop. When I'm working with my partner, Belz, if a perp starts running, I'm jumping over fences and bouncing off the hoods of cars. I'm more or less the muscle, the henchman for the whole crew. Even when Chris gets out of pocket, sometimes the writers have me trying to tame Elliot's anger by getting in his face.

I love working with Mariska. She's a real pro, cool as hell—and hilarious. When I'm doing scenes with Chris it can get explosive, two hard-asses butting heads. With Belzer, I get to roll my eyes and say sarcastic shit. Our writers give me a lot of good one-liners to use on his ass. Belz and me are more like a traditional comedy team within the boundaries of a cop show.

With a truly ensemble cast, depending on the writing of a given episode, any one of us can take the reins and run with it. Actually, that's the way that the show's writers shuffle the deck to give people days off. We have another trick of the trade called "tandem episodes" that we'll do if they're trying to shoot a certain number of shows and we don't have enough weeks. It's like cutting a cake in two. They'll take half the crew with one group, half with another, and we'll shoot two shows simultaneously. In that one eight-day period, Mariska and I may be the leading roles in one show, and Chris and Belz will do another show. Someone will cover for us, saying, "Fin is in court testifying," but that's just because I'm working on another set full-time.

I've had a bunch of episodes where I get the starring role—and it works. The writers have written some great pieces based around Fin and his son, who came out of the closet, which Fin had a hard time accepting. I also had an episode where I was butting heads with Ludacris. In real life, 'Cris is my man, and we had fun on the set, me playing detective and him playing a young cold-blooded murderer. I had another starring role recently in a show about murders among different immigrants in New York, all of whom had so-called "anchor babies" to gain U.S. citizenship. I can carry the weight if they ask me to be the star. If they gave me an episode where I'm the lead and I didn't pull it off, trust me, they wouldn't write one again.

Like making records, acting can be repetitious. You're in there until you get the right take, say your lines spot-on, but as an actor you get to walk away from it. I don't worry about lighting the scene, or editing it, or the background noise of some jet taking off from La Guardia ruining the shot. It's almost like when I'm a vocalist, making a record; in the best case, I walk into the studio, my producer already has the track up, I step in the vocal booth and do my thing. If that track ain't happening, he'll keep playing tracks until I say, "That's hot." And then I'll spit my lyrics, bounce, he'll call me up later on say, "Yo, Ice. I got the mix. Come down and listen."

When I show up for work on the *SVU* set, they've got the set lit, all the extras in place, I just walk in, say my lines, and walk away. Then magically—at least from my perspective—a few weeks later it appears on NBC: Wednesday nights.

In episodic TV, we always say "You're at the mercy of the script." Your day all depends on how heavily your character is written that week. A network television show takes eight days to shoot one episode and, when you add two days for the weekend, you're shooting three episodes a month. One episode of *SVU* will have about forty-two to fifty scenes. That's one ep. You could be in forty-eight scenes if you're Chris or Mariska; you could be in ten scenes if you're me.

But then I'm not getting paid what Chris or Mariska get paid. They're number one and two on the call sheet; I'm number five. If you take a job as a co-star on a TV show, you know from the jump that your workload is lower. If I shoot for eight days, I might shoot five scenes one day, five scenes the next day and then get the other six days off. Or I could shoot a scene a day over those eight days. Mercy of that script.

What a lot of people don't understand about episodic television is that you're not getting paid more when you act in more scenes and less when you're in fewer scenes. They sign you for the season—just like an NBA player. So over the course of those twenty-three episodes, you're going to get the same check even if you're not in an episode at all. Since you can't break out and do a movie or another long-term project, the network still has to pay you a salary; they're buying you and locking you down for the year.

Frankly, I'm glad I'm not the star of every show like I was on *Players.* As cool as Fin is, I think if he was on-screen too much, people would get tired of the character.

It was the same for me in the early days of my hip-hop career. One time when we were doing this big show in New York with Whodini as the headliners, and I was doing my set right before them, I'll never forget, I told Jalil Hutchins, "Yo, one day I'll be up here. I'll be getting top-billing." He pointed at the middle of the poster and said, "Yo man, it's safer *there*." I knew exactly what he meant. If you're the middle act rather than the headliner and the show's a big hit, you can take some of the credit. But if the show's a flop, you just blame it on the bigger names. That's my same position on *SVU*. If the show's a big hit, I get some of the credit; if it bombs, I say, "Okay, but I wasn't the star!"

THE BIGGEST IRONY of my life for the past ten years is that more people recognize me for playing Fin, this street-wise NYPD detective, than remember the whole "Cop Killer" controversy. Cops are now some of my biggest fans. You find that police in the real world are just like normal people—the cops I meet who are in their twenties today are way too young to remember "Cop Killer." Even during the heat of that madness, a lot of police went out of their way to prove to me that they weren't the cop I was singing about, that they were by-the-book officers, not some rogue cops engaged in police brutality.

After landing these gigs in *New Jack City* and *Law & Order,* of course, there's always going to be dumb people out there saying, *Ice, first you're killing police, now you're playing cops. What's up with that?*

Man, shut the fuck up. You stuck on stupid? I'm *acting,* dude. I am not a cop. I've never arrested nobody. I've never read anybody their Miranda rights or slapped them in cuffs.

Check it—this is something I just was discussing with the inmates in Sing Sing when I went there to talk with them. A few years back, I was asked to give the commencement address for the guys behind the wall who'd graduated from university—cats there were getting bachelor's and master's degrees. And we recently went back to Sing Sing to do a follow-up. Most of these guys were lifers, or doing twenty-five-year, thirty-year, forty-year bids. We were chopping it up, exchanging game, swapping war stories. Because that's where I really get information from. If you're in business, it doesn't help you much to talk to someone who's been in business one year. You need to talk to someone who's been in business for thirty years.

We're talking about haters, and one of these hard rocks lays it on me:

"Yo, Ice: All these muthafuckas givin' you shit about playing a cop, trust me, they *use* the cops. All these muthafuckas, all these gangstas, they all use the cops. So fuck that old bullshit—that's posturing and posing. That's just them trying to make themselves look good at your expense. Don't sweat it. Real muthafuckas know that you gettin' cheddar. And ain't an inmate in prison who wouldn't come out and walk on that TV show for a job."

I get this shit all the time. Especially in the age of YouTube, Facebook, and Twitter. "Oh, Ice-T used to be down with the little man," some guy posted online. "Now he's down with the *system.*" I got news for you, dog. The system is a monster. Sooner or later you're going to have to learn how to *work* it. There is no overturning or overrunning the system, you need to learn to manipulate it. Even if you're a gangster, there is still a system.

But you get those haters. Especially when you're an entertainer. Pick any name in the public eye like The Rock, Dwayne Johnson, for example. You'll get these people saying, "Remember The Rock? He was a bad-ass in wrestling but he went soft. Now he does corny kids' movies." Well, check it, idiot—when The Rock was wrestling that was a *character,* too, same way he's playing a superhero or a hockey player in *The Tooth Fairy.* But I try to remember what my mother was always saying back in Summit:

People are stupid.

Real talk.

MAKING THE TRANSITION to the regimented schedule of network TV was rough at first. I was used to the freedom of my life in L.A., running my own record label, calling my own shots, doing concerts on my schedule, and taking movie roles if I was feeling the script. And this might sound crazy, but I honestly don't think I could have developed and sustained a successful career on a network drama if I didn't understand the world of pimpin' and hoin'.

See, the pimp game often translates into the broader world. It's like this: Either you work for somebody or you have them working for you. Now I work for NBC. I don't get the lion's share of the money. I don't make a fraction of what that corporation makes. But I'm happy to do it. I love the gig.

All of us who work in the entertainment business brag on who we work for. "I'm on NBC—Dick Wolf's a legend in this game." "Well, I'm on ABC—we've been number one for years." That's like hoes bragging on their pimps. Yeah, I brag on Dick Wolf. Brag on his reputation. I don't care who you are: Everybody wants to work for the flyer pimp.

I had dinner with Dick Wolf recently in Monte Carlo. I'm not going to front: I was *excited* to sit down with the boss. The man is the man. Sometimes you're lucky. You've got a good pimp. Dick Wolf is cool; he don't whoop me. But don't get it twisted. Don't mistake what it really is—*ever.* If you're not bringing home the lion's share of the check, in a sense, you're hoin'. The key thing is that you don't mistake pimpin' for hoin'. When you hoin' *know* that you hoin'.

One of the primary rules in pimpin' is that you never treat a ho better than the money she brings in. When I had a record deal with Warner Bros. and they were rubbing my neck, telling me how I was the bomb— when Prince walks in, all of a sudden, they'll throw my fucking ass out and the platinum records on the wall will *magically* change to Prince records. All that rubbing of the neck, sweet-talking, bullshitting—yo, that's pimpin'.

I've got the same situation with my employers at NBC Universal. Does NBC really love me? Or does it just love the money I'm bringing in? If I stopped bringing in money, man, they wouldn't even accept my phone calls.

Here's one real jewel from the game. Pimps and hoes don't fall in love, they *make love.* I like to use the strip club example because most men won't cop to having been with a hooker, but they will admit they've been to the strip club. When you're in the club, that girl giving you lap dances, looking into your eyes, doesn't love you. She's *making love* to you. Your dumb ass thinks she loves you and you give her all your money. Sorry. She doesn't give a shit about you, dog.

The big bosses at NBC don't love me; they make love to me. They act like they love me because my fucking show is making money. I'm putting millions of dollars into their bank account. I'm a top-shelf ho, but I'm still a ho.

But, dig—all actors in Hollywood are hoes, as long as they're making the studios and networks money. If you hear some studio executives saying, "Oh, Megan Fox is *hot!*" they don't want to fuck her; they want to know how many guys will pay ten bucks to come to the theater to see her. She's valuable only in as much as she can make them some paper.

I'm not naïve enough to think they actually *care* about any of us. We could drop dead tomorrow; they don't give a fuck. Oh, they'll cry, all right. But the only thing they'll cry over is the money they lost.

Now when you blow up to the level of Will Smith or Tyler Perry, when you run your own successful production company, then you start to pimp yourself. That's where the real Hollywood power is.

If you understand the essence of that game, you won't get caught out there. You won't start catching feelings. Sure, it may be cynical. Cold-blooded. But for me the value of understanding the pimp game is seeing life—all shapes and forms of human interaction—for what it *truly* is, not what you might wish it to be.

ONE THING I'VE LEARNED from straddling two worlds: Hollywood is *way* more gangster than the streets. Hollywood is way colder. Way more vicious. When I first started doing TV and movies, I never saw people get fired the way they do in show business. I never saw the coldness of the producers. They just don't care about anybody. I suppose it's because they don't deal with the same ramifications as you do on the streets; they can hide behind attorneys and lawsuits. It's a whole other set of rules.

With just a glance or a nod from the boss on the set, a producer will get his ass fired. The next day—*boom*—there's a new producer sitting in his chair. The gangster of it is: *I'm not even gonna fire you, dude. You won't even know it's coming.* The boss is smiling the whole time, acting like everything's cool. In the street, we call that rocking somebody to sleep.

I've learned so much hard-core gangsterism from show business. As a black street gangster, if I don't like you, trust me, you'll *know* it. That's something the Italian mob had over us: Black people often have a problem disguising our anger.

It comes down to this. The higher you go up the mountain, the colder it gets. I've been around some of the most ruthless gangsters in the streets of South Central L.A., but I've never seen anything like Hollywood's gangsterism. In the studios, they're dealing with billions of dollars. On the streets, you're dealing with hundreds of thousands of dollars. When cats are dealing with billions of dollars, anybody—I mean, *anybody*—is expendable.

PART SIX

ICEBERG FAMILY VALUES

"IF YOU'RE HAVING GIRL PROBLEMS
I FEEL BAD FOR YOU, SON
GOT NINETY-NINE PROBLEMS
BUT A BITCH AIN'T ONE."
—"99 PROBLEMS"

14.

MONOGAMY IS THE BOMB. Having one steady relationship—yes, *being in love*—that's what turns me on. People trip when they hear that because they're so conditioned to that idea of Ice-as-player that was an early part of my showbiz image. But I've always been into having one serious relationship.

I live by the code: *One down bitch is worth ten funky hoes.*

Even at the height of my rap career, I never felt the need to boost my ego with a bunch of women swarming around me. These days, whenever I see a guy with a gang of girls—like a neon sign announcing to the world that he's a player—I know he's really a trick. Probably a dude with low self-esteem. He may *think* he's a player; but he's a trick because he's paying for all those women. No guy on this earth is handsome enough, sexy enough, charming enough that a bunch of girls are going to hang around him trying to suck his dick just because his dick is that good. Now and again, even an average dude may get *two* girls to fight over him, but not eight, nine, ten chicks. Don't get it twisted. The dude is paying for sex, in some form or fashion, whether it's the cash, the lifestyle, the parties, whatever—it's coming out of his pocket. If that is what he chooses to do, and if he's got the ends to do it—yo, have a blast, man. But again, own that shit. Know what you are: You ain't no player. You a trick.

Most people want to be chosen by a mate for their character. They want to get chosen for what's inside them. And most men—even *real* players—eventually want that one woman they can call "my wife."

Let me give you one more insight from the pimp's code. When a guy decides to get out of the game and get married, true players respect that. What a player will say is, "Just speak on it." Meaning don't come around here with your girl, treating her like shit, acting like you don't care about her, then get pissed when one of the homeys cracks on her.

I don't care where you're from, what gangster nation you claim, real players are going to respect your woman. You just have to make it clear. *This is my wife. This is the mother of my children. I love her.* Then it's hands-off. Men of all stripes are going to respect that. When I was in the game, I remember guys doing that all the time. Sometimes we'd met the chick before, but they'd reintroduce her as "my wife" to make sure we got it. Come up and say, "Yo, this is Cherelle—no, maybe I didn't do that right. This is my *wife.* I love her." And all the guys have to respect that reintroduction. Because there's a different way you treat a guy's wife than you treat some girl who's hanging out with him who's some party chick or another number in his phone book.

DARLENE WAS ASSOCIATED with my career for so long. Even today—ten years into my relationship with Coco—I constantly get asked about Darlene. Darlene was the first long-term relationship in my life.

When I came out of the Army I hooked up with Darlene. It was great between us for years. For more than a decade. Everything was cool. She was up front in my career, she appeared on all my album covers, was in all my videos. As I said, my whole ethos as far as the rap game was not to portray anything fake. Darlene was a natural bombshell and everyone knew it. She was an integral part of the promotion of my album *Power* because one of the record's themes was the power of sex. Darlene developed her own loyal fan base after that. I always referred to her as my wife, although we weren't officially married.

And she was always ready to ride with me, even when the heat on me was most intense. I'll never forget the time I went on *Oprah*—I was the first rapper she ever had on her show. But it wasn't one of those "feel good" sessions O's known for now. This was like a firing line, with all these angry women and critics like Tipper Gore and Juan Williams— now a big name political commentator on Fox—ganging up on me for the profanity and vulgarity they saw in my lyrics. It was me and my man Jello Biafra on the panel and at some point, everyone was going off on me on my use of the word "bitch."

Darlene stood up in the audience, came right to my defense, and checked them.

"When he calls a bitch a *bitch,* then she is a bitch," she said. "When he uses 'bitch' *I* don't turn around. . . . He's not saying all women."

Darlene's cut like that. She's mad loyal. She is the mother of my son, which is a much bigger deal to me than any marriage license.

Our relationship was my first attempt to hold a family together. I grew up an orphan, so I wanted to be there for Little Ice. I was more stable at that time than when LeTesha was growing up. Things were going well—as well as they'd ever gone financially. I was recording hit albums and doing big-budget movies. We had a beautiful house in Sunset Plaza, a Bentley, sports cars, all the entrapments of fame. By any measure, I was doing well. But sometimes you hit a point in your career where you have to go full circle, when you have to start at the beginning again.

I often say: "Love isn't looking somebody in the eyes—it's two people looking out in the same direction." And the direction my career was taking at the time meant I suddenly had to go out and do rap and rock tours again. That's when me and Darlene began to grow apart.

We never had a bad relationship. We just drifted, lost the energy, lost the spark. What I learned from that relationship is this: Yeah, it's true that absence makes the heart grow fonder. But *too* much absence makes you not even need each other; you start to design a life without that other person. With me touring, being away from the home—gradually and unconsciously—we created two separate lives. It was never tense or stressful. In fact, it was a very comfortable arrangement.

At the end of the relationship, I was out of the house more than I was home. I was having more fun going out with my friends. Darlene and I weren't clubbing anymore. I'd be away for weeks, sometimes months; maybe just popping back home with my suitcases for a day at a time.

Relationships with people in the entertainment industry are difficult. You've got to stay completely communicative with that person. This sounds like a cliché but it's true: You've got to stay best friends.

Then I ended up going to New York to do *Law & Order,* and that was a big jump. I had to physically leave Cali and get a new place in New York. Darlene had her own life with friends, family, and Little Ice in school out in L.A. So we weren't a family unit anymore; we were living our separate lives.

At some point during my first few months in New York, I realized what was happening. I couldn't kid myself anymore.

"You know, baby, we're not really together," I said. "You're seeing other people. I'm seeing other people. We're holding this facade together for the kid. Let's just break up as man and wife. But we can keep it together for the kid, because we both love Little Ice. Let's do this. But let's not become enemies. That's only going to hurt him."

We had to do it like that. We were civilized with each other. We weren't angry. We weren't bitter. We actually never fought, screaming back and forth with accusations and recriminations. "You did that!" "No, you did this!" None of that bullshit that you hear about so much in divorces. There was dirt on both sides of the fence. It was more like, "Look, we're not living like we're married. We're living like we're single. So why don't we just make that official?"

We broke up. She stayed in L.A., and I was still in New York City. This was really hard on Little Ice. He was eight years old at the time. But he wasn't used to seeing me around anyway. For much of his childhood, I was gone for extended periods.

I did the single thing in New York for more than a year and that wasn't much fun. I'd been single before, when I was younger. But I'd never been single and *famous.* And I didn't realize how some of these chicks are hunting money. They're targeting. They're focused. They're out to *hit* you.

For a long time, I'd been studying Sharon Osbourne—and when *The Osbournes* came out on MTV, I was hooked. I'd always loved Ozzy. He was one of the first rock stars I connected with back when I was a teenager, so now I was watching this older Ozzy, muttering, mumbling, stumbling around his mansion—looking lost half the time. I sat shaking my head. Does this motherfucker even know he's on TV? Sometimes it wasn't clear that he understood there were cameras following him.

And then I realized it was all Sharon: Sharon running Ozzfest, running this reality TV show, Sharon running Ozzy's day-to-day life. I don't think any guy can look at Sharon and not respect her hustle. I mean, she holds that family together. She holds down her own career *and* Ozzy's career. When it's time for Ozzy to perform somewhere, she basically aims him at the stage, gives him a shove and he screams—

"*Yeah . . . !*"

Ozzy is great at what he does and Sharon allows him to do him.

In my life, I've got the similar strengths and weaknesses. I'm great at what I do. I'm great at performing. I'm great at making money. I've learned how to turn my hustler's eye for opportunity and apply it to the show business game. But I'm essentially an artist. When it comes to all the details, the more mundane side of business and personal life, I'm not real good at all.

While I was single in New York, I found myself looking for a woman who would do for me what Sharon Osbourne was doing for my man Ozzy.

I said this in an interview, and Darlene took offense. She took it as me saying that she couldn't do it. After the interview came out, I had a long conversation with my ex about this. "Darlene," I said, "don't misunderstand me. It wasn't *you*. It was me. I never *asked* you to."

And I'm not saying Darlene couldn't have done all the things Sharon does for Ozzy, but I didn't allow her to take that role. I was trying to play the regular male position. As a man your nature is not to want to show any weakness or talk about any serious problems; you just want to hold down the household. Your instinct is to say: "Look, I got this. I got it. Don't ask how much money's in the bank. Don't ask me about the mortgage or the car notes. Even if I'm tight, baby, you can always shop. Just let me be the man."

I expected Darlene to be the mother, hold down the household, keep food in the fridge, and raise Little Ice while I was out busting my ass working. I was on some real old-fashioned shit.

To be honest, I didn't know that there even was another possibility. I couldn't conceive that a guy—a man in entertainment, especially a rock-and-roll dude—could have an equal, a co-pilot, until I saw Sharon Osbourne at work.

IT WAS ABOUT A YEAR after Darlene and I made our breakup official. I was at a video shoot for one of my friends. I was grumpy. Depressed. I'd been single for a while in New York and I wasn't feeling too happy; I didn't trust too many people—especially new women I was meeting.

One of my player buddies, Ricky Ricardo, saw Coco and he introduced her to me as a way to cheer me up. Right off the bat, I was annoyed. When Coco walked up to me, I didn't want to even say hello. In general, I don't like being introduced to girls. I feel like, *Dude, let me do the fishing.* Now that you done walked this chick up to me, am I obliged to be nice to her? So when I met Coco I was standoffish. Just, "Hey, how ya doin'?" The whole time, my back was turned.

She was standing so close that I could smell her perfume. When I turned around, I looked at her teeth: she's got these little perfect Chiclet teeth and, okay, that was stunning. Then I glanced down at her boobs—*Goddamn!* Still, in my head, I started putting her into the white-girl zone, thinking she was superskinny with fake titties. But then I saw the rest of her and thought, *Okay, what the fuck just happened? That chick got a body on her.* I was hooked.

Coco's got these ill Jessica Rabbit measurements. Superhourglass: 39-23-40.

She'd walked off by the time I realized how smoking she was. Then the video was about to start shooting and I approached her again.

"Okay," I said, "I beg your pardon. Earlier when you were introduced to me, I was stunned. I didn't have my words together. Allow me to reintroduce myself. My name is Ice."

"I know. I'm Coco." I picked up right away that she's from the Valley; she's got that real soft Valley Girl voice.

"Coco," I said, "you're drop-dead gorgeous."

"Thank you."

For the video shoot I had on a red snakeskin suit. Red gators. Black fedora. I never looked more like a pimp. And as always, being dressed like a pimp has me spittin' game like a pimp.

"Would you ever consider dating a gangsta rapper?"

She thought about it for a second. "Well, if he's nice . . ."

"Baby, you take the 'n' off 'nice' you get 'Ice.'"

I know it sounds like a scripted line, but honestly, ain't nobody ever hit me with that opening before. I wouldn't even say that in a lyric— "Yo, I'm nice, take away the 'n' . . ." Nah. I just freestyled it. I think the pimp gods sent me that crazy-ass line.

She burst out laughing. Then I qualified the customer. "I mean, am I *bothering* you here? Are you *married*? Is your *boyfriend* here?"

"No, it's all good," she said, giving me the green light.

We started kicking it. Coco told me she was a swimsuit model, bouncing between L.A., Vegas, and Arizona. She'd done some work for *Playboy*. We were flirting, the banter was good, but then I put the brakes on the vibe.

"Cool," I told her, "but I don't need just another number."

Honestly, I wasn't sure what I was looking for. I wasn't looking for a quick hookup and I wasn't looking for a relationship. I'd just come out of a fourteen-year relationship with Darlene. I didn't want to get back into that; the breaking up and drama wasn't something I was ready for. On the other hand, I can't front—Coco was hot.

Fortunately, she'd been out there already. She'd been with the rich guys, been with the broke guys, been with the nice guys and the bad boys—she'd seen it all. Coco wasn't looking for another number, either. Still, I had to take it slow. You can't come right out tell a chick you just met—no matter how smoking—that you're really looking for a girl to hold you down, to be your co-pilot in life.

People think Coco is the ultimate party chick, but she's not. She's much more of a stay-at-home-and-scrub-the-kitchen-sink-type chick. I found that out a few weeks after I met her. She came to New York with one of her friends to visit me. We were hanging out one afternoon, watching a game on TV. And while I'm sitting there with my friend Mickey, for some reason, Coco starts to vacuum my house. Came through the whole crib, getting the dust out of every nook and cranny. After she vacuumed, my carpet looked brand-new. I looked at Mickey and said, "What the fuck is going on here?"

That's a lesson it took me a while to learn. When a woman wants you, she'll move on you domestically. If you're dating a chick and she won't pick up one of your socks, she doesn't give a fuck about you. She just wants a meal. But once a girl starts cooking for you, reorganizing your clothes closet, it means she wants you. Too often men don't have the first clue about what's going through a woman's mind. When a woman comes over and starts vacuuming and folding the towels in your bathroom, she's planning on moving in.

We had a good weekend. But we were still in the casual dating phase. The next time she came back for about twelve days. This was like a test run going full throttle in "Ice mode." She came to the set of *Law & Order;* she came with me while I gave a college lecture; she went to an Ice-T hip-hop show—basically, she had to run at my speed.

Like Rakim says, "No time to comb your hair, baby, brothers is bustin' at me." I didn't plan it that way—that was just my week's schedule—but it was a little exercise in keeping up with me. She passed with flying colors. She didn't want to be left at home for a minute. If I had to get up at five in the morning to get to the set, she got up at five in the morning. She was getting ready in twenty minutes; she knew how to change her vibe from dressing sexy-fly for the rap concert to the more conservative lecture circuit to being stylish but understated on the set of *SVU.*

The days flew by. When it came time to head back home, she looked sad. We were already at the airport gate.

"What's up?" I said. "You don't want to go home?"

"No."

We stood at the gate in silence for a while.

"Okay, then," I said. "We'll have to take this to the next level."

When she was back West, I spent a few days in a haze. I was trippin'. I'd never been in this situation in my life. Because now I was stationed in New York, working a job with long-ass hours, and I liked a chick on the other side of the country. I couldn't bounce—my shooting schedule on *Law & Order* had me tethered to New York City.

So I called Coco and told her to come back to New York. And this time to bring a lot more clothes.

I didn't plan on her becoming my "Sharon Osbourne" right away. She just naturally started to handle all my daily scheduling, organization, and communications.

At that point, Sean E. Sean was acting as my personal assistant. He was living at my crib, running everything day-to-day. About a week after Coco came out to New York, I saw Sean packing his bags in the spare bedroom.

"What up, homey?"

"Yo, man, I'm *out*," Sean said. "You don't need me no more. She *got* this."

THIS WAS THE FIRST TIME in my life when I entered into a relationship with a woman fully *knowing* what I wanted, what I expected, and most important, how to communicate it to her.

In life, I've learned, whatever you want from your woman, know that's what you want. Then fucking tell 'em. If you want a girl that brings home girls, tell 'em. You may not get the girl you want but *eventually* you'll find a girl who'll do that. Might as well be upfront and say, "Baby, I'm looking for a chick that's gonna bring home chicks." But you better know that's what you really want because that's a whole fucking world in its own. Dealing with two girls or three girls—all that bullshit. Don't get me wrong—that's fun to do when you're single. That will *not* work in a relationship.

People think of Ice and Coco as always pushing the limits. People think we party all the time, but practically the only time they snap pictures of us is when we're at some red-carpet premiere or we're clubbin' and she's got on some fluorescent-pink micromini and matching stilettos. Yo, that's how everybody dresses when they're clubbin'.

Like I told her from the jump, I didn't need another number. I didn't need another party chick. I needed a woman full-time in my life *and* in my career. I wanted that Sharon Osbourne, that co-pilot, but I'd never tried it out before. This was a complete one eighty for my mental. I was hardwired to feel that having someone help me like that would make me less strong.

It didn't take long for Coco and me to start working together before I realized how much I *loved* it. I've got a pretty short attention span for the mundane details of life. I'm the type of dude that feels I don't really need to know what's happening three Sundays from now—I don't need to know what's happening *next* Sunday. When I wake up in bed next to Coco, I just need to know what I have to do today; and then by the middle of the day, let me know what's happening tomorrow. I tell her to leak it to me, bit by bit, once I'm already up and rolling. By now she knows what I'll do, what I won't do; and she knows how to diplomatically decline offers that I just don't have time for.

The biggest problem when we started working together was my communication style. A lot of times I would chop her head off. It wasn't personal; it's the way I get sometimes. I can be abrupt as fuck. I was used to telling Sean E. Sean how to get shit done in as few words as possible. And we've been boys for so long, we'd dispense with the niceties like "please" and "I very much appreciate it." I'd be abrupt with Coco and then I'd see it affecting her. I'd see her puppy-up, thinking I was angry with her.

"No, baby, that's just the tone I use when I'm in business mode."

Over time, we worked out some codes. Now we've got "on the clock" and "off the clock." That means during the day we're doing business, and a lot of the formalities, the politeness, just ain't in the mix. I'll say, "Yo Coco, call so-and-so," turn around and she's already dialing the cell.

We go off the clock at night, and the formalities and all the respect that's necessary in a marriage comes back. It's hard to be overly polite in business. You gotta just get into it. Get shit done. And being as direct as possible is essential for me. That makes doing business with someone you love an even greater challenge.

Relationship-wise, a lot of times your partner gets into a funky mood, and you'll want to do everything in your power to make your partner happy. You'll try to apologize, try to fix it, but there's nothing you can do about it. Coco and me just say, "Yo, it's not you. I'm dealing with something." A lot of times you just need to cycle through situations; you need thirty minutes to work through the mood and tell your partner not to personalize it.

My earlier relationships were structured different. What I learned was that if you want to be with somebody, you can't let weeks go by where you don't communicate. With Coco, when we're "off the clock," we try to talk all the time.

People are always asking, "What's the thing that holds you guys together?" They think that it's love or sex or companionship. I say "admiration." Love is a great thing but you also have to admire your mate. When I go on one of her modeling shoots, I watch her working and think, "Yo, Coco is the bomb." When I'm rapping or doing my thing as an actor, she says, "That's just Ice—he can do that shit."

I don't mean this to sound too corny, but when you admire your partner, when neither one feels subservient to the other, then you actually feel like teammates. It becomes a real-life Bonnie and Clyde, ride-or-die dynamic. It's tough sometimes in the heat of a relationship to remember that y'all are teammates and not opponents; allies not enemies. A successful marriage is built on the realization that the other person helps the overall situation, that they've got your back no matter what.

With Coco and me both being in the public eye—snapped by paparazzi and eavesdropped on by gossip hounds—we need to approach things as a team. Our moves have to be strategic. We try to plan which one of us would be better for certain things. Even simple shit, like getting a room at a hotel. Who would be better for that task? If there's a guy at the front desk, maybe he'll react better to Coco. If there's a woman, she may react better to me. She might have some hostility to Coco—*Oh, I don't like that bitch. Fuck her.*

We're still players—I mean, we're legit players now—and part of being players is knowing that there's a strength in the feminine side and a strength in the masculine side. Knowing how to use whoever is better for the task. She's much better at answering phones, scheduling meetings, and has better people skills than me. No matter how hard I try to work on it, I'm always very short with people. I don't like phones at all. Maybe it goes back to my days hustling when we looked at every phone call as a liability. When you're hustling you try not to say shit that could be recorded or intercepted by the cops. And as so many gangsters found out, being too chatty on the phone can get your fucking ass locked up for life.

PEOPLE ALWAYS ASK COCO and me, "How do you keep it hot? How do you keep things exciting in the bedroom?"

It's very simple. I have to find out what turns her on and I've got to be willing to do it. And she has to ask me what I like and be willing to do it.

If you find somebody you're attracted to, you're going to have to tell them *exactly* what buttons to push. You can't expect them to know it. If you've both been through serious relationships previously, remember that what worked in the past isn't necessarily going to work in your current relationship. If you're willing to give that person what he or she needs, your sex life will always be good.

If your mate wants something but you're not willing to give it, do you think he or she *stops* wanting it? Hell no. You'd better recognize that this is something that your partner will keep looking for—outside the relationship if necessary.

Hopefully, you'll find someone who can accommodate everything you need.

One thing about Coco: She's very in touch with her sexuality. I don't understand why a lot of women see that as a fault; I see that sexiness as her power. The details of our relationship and how we've made it work—giving each other satisfaction, happiness, and peace for ten years now—is enough to fill a whole other book.

IT'S NOT ALWAYS EASY to have two interlocking show business careers but it helps to remember one thing: At the end of the day, we've got one bank account. If that account is fat, we livin'. If it's short we ain't. We both have to generate money. Coco is not one of those chicks who feels comfortable with the man making most of the money. That's why she's got a clothing line and runs her website, because she likes to put money in the kitty. I respect that. She even appeared on *Law & Order* and landed a couple of small speaking roles. And it wasn't like I was angling for her to get any parts. The producers would be looking to cast a chick and they'd say—"No, she can't be too skinny, can't look like a fashion model. She should be blond, fit, and have curves—you know, like Coco."

And they'd point at Coco, since she's almost always by my side on the set. One time, instead of saying, "You know, like Coco," a producer said, "Hey, why don't we just use Coco for this?"

She made me run lines with her for days in our crib. She rehearsed her lines about a hundred times more than I've ever rehearsed mine.

We had an episode with a mixed martial arts theme, and Coco had the part as UFC fighter Forrest Griffin's girlfriend. She played a gold digger who was just into Forrest for his dough. She was great. I teased her about it, too: She played the gold digger part a little *too* well, as a matter of fact!

COCO WAS THE FIRST WOMAN I dated that Little Ice ever met. I'd seen other women before Coco, but I never felt that another woman was the right one to meet my son. People are funny like that. Take a single woman with children; she can date a lot of guys before one of them gets to meet her kids. And I was the same way with Little Ice.

But luckily we did it the right way. Darlene was mad cool. She briefed Little Ice before his first trip to stay with us. She said, "Look, when you're with your dad and Coco, the one thing they *don't* need is to hear all about me." And Coco's such a sweetheart, they just hit it off. Little Ice knows karate and the first day, I'll never forget, they were stretching, limbering up together.

Now that's tough to do, but it takes three adults—Darlene, Coco, and me—to make that work. I made that clear to Darlene from the jump. Look if you and me become enemies, then who's going to lose? The dude. Little Ice is the one who's going to take all the collateral damage.

Not to say everything's roses. Like others, my ex and I still have our moments when we get into it. But it can't affect our son. We know we've got to solve it, we've got to get it together so he doesn't take it to heart.

Boundaries are essential if you're going to make this kind of situation work. Coco doesn't try to play the mom role. Never. She doesn't try to discipline him. Doesn't get in his face. If Little Ice and me are having conflict, or Little Ice and Darlene are having conflict, she steers clear of it. Coco knows she's *my* partner. So if she has any issues with my son, she's very careful to relay it through me. And then I bring it to Ice.

MATTER OF FACT, I had to *bring* it to Little Man not long ago. Ice lives full-time with his mother in Los Angeles. I'm the first to say Darlene does a tremendous job, making sure his grades are tight, that he walks a straight line, stays out of trouble. I see him as much as I can, but with my shooting schedule during the *Law & Order* season, it can get hectic. When I'm not shooting, Little Ice comes to visit us every time he gets a break from school. Last year—spring break of his junior year—he came out to stay with Coco and me at our house in Arizona.

One night during that break, Darlene started blowing up my cell late at night. She sounded shaken up.

"What's wrong, D?" I asked.

"They just towed Ice's car out of the driveway."

"What? Police?"

"Yeah."

"You sure it was the cops?"

"It was the cops. They came to talk to me. I wasn't here, but the neighbors saw them hooking up Ice's car."

Darlene was concerned, of course, but not too worried. She figured it was either a misunderstanding or something involving unpaid tickets. But knowing the game, I got concerned.

"Dig, that ain't no traffic ticket bullshit," I said. "The cops do not come and tow your vehicle at night unless that car was involved in a crime."

"What are you talking about?"

"If your car is parked at home, in your own driveway, and the police come to tow it, that can mean only one thing: The car was linked to some serious criminal shit. Let me handle this," I said. "But this ain't a joke. Ice might be coming straight home to you."

Little Ice was psyched up because this was just the start of his vacation in Arizona, so I knew it was going to blow his mind when I got in his face.

"Yo, Ice!" I called out. He came and found me in the living room. I sat him down. "Look, dude, I'm about to talk to you, for real. But before we even talk, I advise you one thing: You better tell me the truth."

"Okay, Dad."

"The truth, you dig?"

"Yeah."

"I'm a fucking career criminal *and* I play the police on TV, so I know how this shit goes. Don't even waste my time or your time with some bullshit."

By now, of course, he's scared as hell. His eyes are darting back and forth, and he's fidgeting with the brim of his fitted ball cap. He's trying to play it off, like he doesn't know what the fuck is going down. But I know he's guilty of something. He couldn't even look me in the eye.

I let him sit there in silence for a long-ass time.

"What's up, Dad?" he said, still playing dumb.

"Just got a call from your moms. The cops just came and towed your car out of the driveway."

"Oh, that must be some old tick—"

"Shut the fuck up and listen. The *only* reason the cops would come to your mom's house at night and tow your car is that a crime was committed involving the car. Now before you say anything else, you just might want to think—take a minute—because I'm gonna wanna know what *exactly* you did in that car."

Another long-ass pause. I could tell he wished he could just scramble up the wall like these little lizards we got all over the yard in Arizona.

I was almost doing my Fin routine, giving a suspect the third-degree in the interview room.

"Now you want to tell me what happened?"

Little Ice sat there, nervous, then started to spill.

"I know what happened," he said. "The other night we were at a party and my friend"—see, it always starts out with some fucking *friend*—"busted into the car parked next to us and stole a laptop."

"Your friend?"

"Yeah, my friend."

"Which friend?"

He told me who and I recognized the kid as this wiseass in his class. I'm getting half the story, but that's cool: I don't get him copping to the break-in or anything, but at least we've established that some criminal shit went down.

The wheels in my hustler's brain are spinning. I already knew that if the cops knew the make, model, and plates on Little Ice's car, that could only mean one thing: He was on film. They had that videotape and they'd seen the whole shit go down, captured the break-in and watched my son and his friends get away in Little Ice's vehicle. Every-fucking-thing is videotaped now in California.

"Maybe you're telling me the whole story," I said. "Maybe you're telling me half the story. I don't really care. But you know what? You probably were videotaped by surveillance cameras, so it's all going to come out in court anyway."

"What're you talkin' about—videotaped?"

"Your car just got towed, dog, and shit's going down. So I'm about to call the detectives and find out what the fuck's up. Anything else you wanna tell me about what your *friend* got into that night?"

"Naw, naw. That's just what happened."

I know his mentality perfectly—I've been this kid. He doesn't want to tell a *syllable* more than he has to.

I called up LAPD and reached the detective who had the case. He told me what I'd suspected: it was a burglary from a car, all the kids were caught on videotape, no ambiguities about it.

"Okay, detective, how do we handle this?"

"I advise you to get an attorney."

This cop ain't giving me no slack and no easy way out. So I hang up, go back and find Little Ice.

"Dig, man, you probably going to have to pack yo' shit 'cause you gonna have to go back to L.A. and handle this."

I called up a defense attorney known for taking criminal cases in Hollywood. I heard he had some other celebrity clients. He'd got some movie star's kid out of a jam—more dumb-ass teenage shit—for breaking into the student store at his college.

The lawyer jotted down all the details and then he called the cops. The LAPD gives him the straight dope—since there wasn't any violence, it wasn't *that* serious. And if we could get the stolen material back, return it all to the owner of the car, we might even be able to make the case disappear.

I asked the attorney if he could handle it. "Yeah," he said, then asked me for a ten thousand dollar retainer.

That's American justice for you—as long as there's no violence (and sometimes even if there is)—if you got enough paper, you can smooth over almost any legal jam. The most important thing, the lawyer tells me, is that we keep this off Ice's permanent record.

"You guys are going to have to follow my instructions to T," he tells me.

For ten G's, I expected this cat to know what the fuck he was doing. I tracked down Little Ice and yanked him off the fucking Xbox. "Look man, they want that laptop back," I said. "They want anything else you might have stolen. Return all that shit and maybe—maybe—they can make this go away. Other than that, you're looking at probably a year in jail."

Little Ice froze: freaked the fuck out.

"Might as well come clean now. Is there anything else that came up missing out of that car?"

There was about sixty dollars cash in some Asian currency that these knuckleheads took just for the hell of it. And then Little Ice was mumbling . . . "Yeah, well, Dad . . . I took a tennis racket . . ."

"A fuckin' tennis racket?"

Once my son told me he stole a tennis racket, I understood the whole game.

"So you was just tryin' to be down? A tennis racket? What the fuck you need with a tennis racket? I'll *buy* you any tennis racket if you want. Naw, I know. That was you just tryin' to prove you could be down with your boys."

I'm getting heated now. The father in me is pissed. But the ex-criminal in me remembers all too well that peer pressure I used to hear back in South Central: Nigga, you scared of money? You scared of money? And how many of my homeys got locked up doing serious bids because—just like Little Ice—they was trying to be down.

I was pacing in our living room, mulling over our next move when I noticed Ice, sitting on the sofa, staring at me with this strange, wide-eyed expression.

"What?" I said.

"Naw, nothing, Dad."

"Spit it out, man."

Finally he said what was on his mind.

"How'd *you* get away with it?"

I almost lost it—*the fuckin' balls on this kid!*—wanting me to give him pointers on the game. I sat down next to him on the sofa and stared him dead in the eye.

"You want to know how I got away with it? Okay. Number one, you fuckin' dumb-ass: You never commit a crime in your own car. Let's start with that. Two: When I was doin' it, they didn't have surveillance cameras mounted on every fucking palm tree in California. Three: I didn't have a *rich father* who could buy me the shit. I don't know if there's a God up there, but if there is, then He knows you knew what the fuck you was doing, and you should get caught. How'd I get away with it? I don't fuckin' know. I think I got a pass because I was poor, broke, and halfway-homeless—idiot!"

I started laying it on him now. Giving him the scared-straight treatment—Iceberg edition.

"You go to jail, Ice, remember this: You're privileged. Muthafuckas don't respect the privileged in jail. Plus, you're Mexican and black. So you don't have a car to be in: Who the fuck you gonna be with? Niggas ain't going to cosign. The *éses* ain't going to take you. Sorry, man, you're royally *fucked.*"

He was on the verge of real tears now.

I said, "What'chou weigh now, son—'bout a buck-thirty? You might want to do some pushups 'cause you're light in the ass and you're gonna end up someone's bitch in there."

I ended up having to put him back on a plane from Phoenix to L.A. One of his friends—that smart-ass kid—wouldn't come in to 'fess up. He was trying to play hardball. Probably because he was the supposed mastermind of this shit. The third one is one of Ice's closest friends, a pretty good kid whose moms ended up talking to the other kid's parents.

Ice thought he was on some "code of the streets" shit; he didn't want to spill too much; didn't want his friends to see him as a snitch.

"Man," I said. "Let me tell you about the code of the streets. You done *told* your mother. Once you've told your mother, your mother can't snitch. Your mother is the *mother.* She doesn't stand by that code-of-the-streets shit. That's her job: She tells the other parents."

We get the smart-ass kid and his parents to come in to talk to the detectives. But the biggest deal was now we had to recover the laptop—that thing made the case grand larceny—but the knuckleheads were playing hot potato. The laptop was over at some other kid's house, and these guys were so terrified they didn't want to even touch it anymore. Afraid of fingerprints or some shit, even though they'd already handled the motherfucker.

We've only got twenty-four hours to get the computer back. I reach out to some of my original crime partners from South Central. Takes a minute but we get a lead on where the kid holding the computer lives. Then I put Sean E. Sean on the case. So Sean E. Sean—all swoll-up with his prison muscle from his most recent bid—shows up at the kid's door unannounced.

"Dig, homey, we need that laptop."

Boom—the kid hands it right over.

You have to understand—Sean E. Sean's taking a big risk even running this recovery mission for me. Sean's got two strikes already—two felony sentences. So if he gets caught even transporting that stolen computer, he can go back to the pen for *life*. No joke.

Luckily, Sean knows how to move in stealth. He gets me the stupid laptop, we get it to Ice's moms, and Darlene turns the laptop in to the police.

I had to buy Little Ice a nice new suit. Darlene had to go with him to the hearing. I knew it was probably all going to get squashed. But I've already given this attorney the ten-grand retainer, so I told him to make my kid sweat a bit. Let him know what he's really looking at. Ice ended up getting a one-year probation, but it took a good six months to clear the legal bullshit up.

THE YEAR-LONG PROBATION didn't matter much to him. I don't think he really woke up—really felt how he'd fucked up—until the end of his senior year. It wasn't just the car break-in, he was distracted and slipping.

Little Ice is smart as fuck. He's smart enough that he only has to show up at class to get a B. If he does the reading and applies himself, he can get the A. He was slacking and got caught out there. Adolescence hit him in the head. At the start of the year, he had a girlfriend and they were both getting great grades; she'd do the homework with him. But they broke up and once he got single, he found out he was fly, found out he was slick, and he starting hanging out with his dudes. Hanging with his bum-ass friends, breaking into fucking cars to snatch up laptops and tennis rackets.

That's one thing I've learned about parenting. Your kids need to feel it. Not hear it. *Feel* it. By the end of twelfth grade, he had decent grades, but ended up five credits short on graduation. They wouldn't let him walk. It would've been different if he didn't graduate and nobody said nothing. But because he couldn't graduate with his friends, couldn't walk the stage, he hurt. He really felt what I warned him about. Because every friend and uncle and aunt had marked it on their calendar. He had one hundred people—literally—that wanted to come to his graduation. And he had to man-up and tell them he wasn't walking.

He had to stay and re-do summer school English. He had his diploma by mid-July, but he was still bummed out that he didn't get to walk the stage in June. And that's a big moment in any teenager's life. I'd warned him for a long time. "Yo, I'm not the one that's going to feel fucked up, homey. *You* will."

And he did. I saw it in his eyes. You can do all the parenting in the world, but something like that has to happen to them from time to time, something that knocks the wind out of them. And that graduation shit hit him hard. I know that it sucked way more than me bawling him out or punishing him. "Okay, let him just feel that sadness and disappointment," I told Darlene. "Don't say nothin' more."

A few weeks after the graduation he came to me, looking more focused than I've ever seen him.

"Dad," he said. "I'm gonna walk the stage in college."

"All right. Cool. I'll hold you to that."

Little Ice is a good kid—way closer to a ten than a five. But he's got his issues. He's a teenager. It's rough for any teenager these days.

In addition to all the usual pressures on today's kids, he's stuck having a famous father, and everybody he meets gives him that weight of responsibility, reminding him about the shoes he's got to fill. They're testing him all the time, letting him know—*Dude, you're carrying Ice-T's name.*

I don't care how balanced and together you are, that's a heavy weight for any kid to bear.

SINCE I NEVER HAD PARENTS for those difficult years—all that crazed adolescent rabble-rousing shit—I have got to make my own blueprint. I can't follow some parenting manual. Everyone knows I was never an angel, so I've got to live by my own values—Iceberg Family Values.

I've led an unconventional life, so I guess it makes sense I've had to deal with some unconventional parenting problems. Little Ice only recently started giving me headaches, but back in the day, I had way more complicated issues with my daughter, LeTesha. One time, I got a phone call in the middle of the night from the LAPD.

"Is this the residence of LeTesha Marrow?"

"No. Who's asking?"

"We're looking for the parents of LeTesha Marrow."

"What the hell's going on?"

I damn near dropped the phone. This cop starts telling me that my daughter was busted with her boyfriend in a raid on a dope house down in the 'hood. And not only was she busted in the dope house, she was caught in possession of her boyfriend's gun.

"A fuckin' dope house?" I said, half losing my mind. I was never that into the drug game, of course, but I had friends who were big-time dealers. We'd be in the dope house and it was insane what you'd see: Niggas would show up with six-foot lamps, lawn furniture, air-conditioners to trade for drugs. One time we were in a dope house and these fiends came with some huge machine they'd ripped off from a hospital—we found out later it was high-tech equipment that a cardiologist would use. We were all saying, "Where the fuck did you get this?" Crackheads can be some devious, creative motherfuckers. You never know what's going to happen next in a dope spot.

So I considered myself lucky and bailed my daughter out of jail. I knew her boyfriend, some half-assed gangster, was going to advise her how to handle the jam—of course, he'd want her to claim ownership of the pistol—but I had to take charge. The first mission was to get her separated from the boyfriend.

I grabbed her hand tight as soon as I got her bailed out of lockup.

"LeTesha, I don't give a fuck if this is a guy you love, if you think you're going to be together forever," I said. "Fuck all of that. Basically, as far as the cops are concerned, you do not know him. You're just some bitch he met that very day. You ain't nothin' but hood rat to him. You meet, he asks you to hang out. See, if you don't know him, then you don't gotta testify against him. Plus, he ain't gotta corroborate stories with you. You guys just met that day. Can you go along with that? Can y'all stick to that story?"

"Yeah," she said, nodding.

"Now, as for the pistol: You're just *stupid*. You wanted to be down. He asked you to hold it, and you didn't know no better. Got it? You're copping to being a dumb-ass, and that's it. He's taking that gun case."

We talked to her boyfriend and told him the story. He only met my daughter a few hours before the raid. He doesn't even know her real name. And he's copping to ownership of the piece. Dude shrugs at me, acting like a bad-ass. "Yo, that's no problem, Ice."

Then I got my daughter alone, in the passenger seat of my Benz. "Look, Tesha. If you're hanging out with a guy that's got a gun, then he's potentially—fuck 'potentially'—he's *probably* got people after him. You've got to know that the killers that are after him would just as soon kill you to get their point across. Anytime you meet a guy, and he's carrying guns, you do not need to be fucking with him. Period. You're just as much a target as he is. When niggas shoot up the car, they don't say, 'Hold up! Miss the passenger!' They shoot the whole fucking car up.

"That's one lesson you need to know. Secondly, know this: When you're in a dope house and the door gets kicked in, you *pray* to God it's the cops. Because if it's them other motherfuckers, then everybody's dead. All of y'all. So therefore, you don't need to be in none of these spots with none of these guys."

I'm lecturing her, driving her back to her mother's crib, but I'm also hearing another soundtrack in my mind: the B-Side of this record. I know that what she's doing right now is searching out a guy who's like her dad. Even as I'm telling her how she fucked up, I'm trying to come to grips with that. My daughter is always going to search for a guy that's got a hard edge. A guy that's tough, that's cool, that's gangster.

Every other guy she meets, she thinks he's weak. Because she's seen how I handle shit. She's seen her father's get-down. Almost every other boyfriend she had in the past, she'd complain to me, "Daddy, he soft" or "He act like a punk."

I don't really feel like I messed up with Tesha. I lived my life and I don't have any regrets. But I do recognize my dilemma. I don't care who you are as a father, your daughter is going to seek you out. In all your negativity. Whatever you think you are as a husband and as a man, to your daughter, you're her first man. So it's like we always say in the game, *Don't talk about it—be about it.* It doesn't matter what you tell her to do, how to live her life, what to look for in a man. What you portray, your daughter will always—*always*—seek out.

So I have to own that, too.

But now that I've transformed, Tesha's starting to look for guys that are more like the new me rather than the old me. When she was growing up, I was hustling. That's who I was. I was doing dirt every day. She went after those criminal-minded guys. Now that I'm on TV—who the fuck knows? Maybe she'll go after an actor.

TODAY, LETESHA AND I are on great terms. She lives in Atlanta. She's real cool—a hip young lady. A mom with three kids of her own. And she's great with Little Ice. One of her sons is a year younger than Ice, so they hang out, shoot hoops, play videogames together.

I've realized that, as children come into their own adulthood, they understand more about parenthood. About *your* parenthood, your strong suits as well as your shortcomings and mistakes. Of course, the fact that I wasn't around when Tesha was a child hurt her a lot. But as she's grown up, been with guys—and things didn't work out, raising three children by herself—she realized that marriage is a great concept in theory but it doesn't always work. She's going through domestic strife and the struggle of being a single mother, so she understands how complicated these things can be.

Funny enough, LeTesha is the first person I talked to about marrying Coco. I'd never married Tesha's mom, Adrienne; never officially married Darlene, and this was the first time I ever considered formally tying the knot.

I was a bit reluctant to ask her. I thought my daughter might trip, because she's almost exactly the same age as Coco.

"I want to ask your advice about something, Tesha."

"Okay . . ."

My kids aren't used to me calling them up for advice.

"I'm thinking about marrying Coco."

She didn't miss a beat. "If you don't, you're *crazy*. Coco is *fine*." Then after a long pause. "And she's good for you, too, Daddy."

ON THE FAMILY FRONT, I know I've made my share of mistakes. But now I'm just out here trying to make a few more millions so I can leave them all a trust fund and be that patriarch in the portrait over the mantelpiece.

Honestly, I'm starting my family from scratch. I've got my daughter, Tesha, and my son, Little Ice. I've got my wife, Coco—our relationship is now ten years strong—but she's not their mother. That's a complicated family dynamic, I know. But our relationships are probably more close to the average American family than the advertising image of two parents living with their two perfect kids in the 'burbs.

We make it work. I'm happy with Coco. I'm also happy with Darlene. People on the sidelines still ask me why Darlene and me aren't together. And I tell 'em, "This is not a storybook." It starts off like that, but shit happens. Fortunately for us things never got ugly. We didn't have a public breakup.

When you see these celebrity divorce meltdowns, at least one of the two sides has got to *want* to take it public. You've got to *decide* to take it public. If my ex wanted to be in the press and say negative shit about me, she could do it. And they'd eat it up. Page Six and TMZ would have a field day. But you've got to make a decision: Who ends up having to deal with that bullshit? The kid. In the end it would be Little Ice taking all the damage.

My wife's been turning me into more of a family man than I've ever been. I fought it hard at first. When I first got with Coco, I was amazed by how tight she is with her family. She's close with her brother and sister. Her parents are divorced, but they're real cool. They have these regular family meetings to talk out issues. I never had any of that. Like I said, there just wasn't much talking in my household in New Jersey. I never went to Christmas dinners. I always felt like I was an outsider. Over time, I started to enjoy being a loner and built that up as my protective shell.

But Coco recently got me sitting down at Thanksgiving and Christmas dinners with her family. I had such internal resistance to it all. Because when you're a kid and you don't have a tight family unit, you cancel it out. You tell yourself that you don't want it or need it.

Fuck Thanksgiving—that shit's stupid. Fuck Christmas, too. Fuck family. Matter of fact—fuck the world.

That was my attitude for years and years.

And I can't lie: I still have mixed emotions. I like doing the family thing, but I also still hold on to my reluctance to be a part of one, to give up the image I have of myself as a lone wolf. The downside to families is the pain—you expect a lot out of them, and inevitably they let you down.

WHEN YOU GET NAMED ICE it's because you seem to lack emotions. You seem cold to the world. But that coldness was never a negative attribute to me. The way I've always seen it is: Emotions don't really get shit done.

The sooner you learn how to contain emotions and move past them, the sooner you can survive serious situations. When you're in the military you're not allowed to be emotional. You've just got to handle the task. If some shit goes wrong, deal with it. The attitude is not, *Don't cry over spilled milk.* It's, *Don't cry. Period. That's just a wasted emotion.* Same thing in the street; the hustler's life isn't any more emotional than a military dude.

When both of your parents die when you're a kid, when most of your friends die before you're twenty-one—getting killed in the gang wars, OD'ing on drugs—and the rest end up in prison, there's a part of your personality that goes numb. It actually atrophies. For most of my adult life, deep emotions were foreign to me. They were nothing but a liability.

But the strange thing is, now that I'm over fifty I've been getting a lot more open to my feelings. I guess it just had to hit me at the right time. Like a door inside me had to be *ready* to open. You lose the self-absorption you felt as a young man. If there's one thing I don't believe in, it's self-pity. These days, I care more about other people than I do about myself. I still have a pretty cold, detached attitude about my own life—my own daily dramas—but if you want to see me get real emotional, talk to me about the people I love.

PART SEVEN

PEACE AND WAR

"MY LIFE'S BEEN A GREAT STORY

IN THE ULTIMATE WAR

SHOULD I ILL OR DO RIGHT?

MAKE PEACE OR GO RAW?"

—"EXODUS"

15.

HIP-HOP SAVED MY LIFE. That's no bullshit. It was hip-hop that got me out of that negative cycle I was living. If I'd stayed a hustler, I've got no doubt, I'd either be dead or in the pen like so many of my partners.

I was passionate about hip-hop when I first heard it. I remain passionate about it. But today's hip-hop—let me try to be diplomatic—well, we say it "lacks soul." It lacks content. It lacks lyrical depth. It lacks a lot of the elements that made hip-hop so great to us.

Since I've always been a motherfucker who speaks his mind, I'm not shy about telling. This got me into some media static a couple years back with the young rapper Soulja Boy. He was riding his hit "Superman" at the time and someone asked me what I thought of him. I called it like I saw it. To me his music was some kind of bubblegum rap, and during a studio session, I said he was "killing hip-hop."

Looking back, the whole situation was unfortunate. I never meant my comments to be spread so widely or to be taken so seriously. I was in the studio and somebody was getting at me about Soulja Boy and the newer cats in hip-hop. That's like taunting a fighter. Talk shit to an old boxer and you'll most likely hear: "Fuck him, I will bust his ass. I'll rip his fuckin' head off."

There's that same visceral response you get when you talk to an old-school rapper. When you're part of the game, you're intimately connected to it. For me, talking about hip-hop is practically like talking about my kids. The context of my comment was me saying, "Look, we've come all the way from Rakim, Public Enemy, and KRS-One and now—come on, man, nowadays y'all are *bullshittin'*. Man-the-fuck-up. This is wack."

Then I told the young dude, "Eat a dick." That's just an L.A. term meaning "Kiss my ass" or "Shut the fuck up." Nothing more than that. "Eat a dick, nigga." It doesn't mean *suck* my dick. It ain't a literal invitation to perform fellatio. In L.A., you hear "eat a dick" every day.

My comments ended up on a mixtape, Soulja Boy heard them and went and made a YouTube video. He got personal. Looked me up on Wikipedia. Talking about how old I was and all this shit.

"Okay, dude," I said, "you got angry but you decided to get a little bit fly."

So I replied back with my son there—Little Ice is about the same age as the dude—and I tried to clarify my point. I apologized to him. I also told him, "I'm talking about your music, I don't know you. But as a hip-hop G, I feel I have to stand on it."

It touched a raw nerve. Cats throughout the rap world started taking sides. Kanye West jumped to the defense of Soulja Boy, but a gang of rappers like Snoop co-signed with me. The cats that knew me said, "Yeah, that's what Ice and them niggas do! They don't give a fuck! Them niggas been cursing motherfuckers out since day one." But kids that didn't know me thought I was coming off kind of harsh. Not just stating my opinion but *stomping* on the young homey.

In retrospect, I understand: Dude is a child. As a child you don't really have guidance. Maybe he doesn't know about the ground-breaking artists who laid the foundation for him. Maybe he doesn't know enough to pay homage to those men. Or maybe he isn't *capable* of making better music. I mean, it's not his *intent* to destroy hip-hop.

Soulja Boy doesn't know me from a can of paint. Good luck with his career. Good luck to everything he's trying to do.

But as a G, being emotionally invested in something I had a hand in creating, I want the art form to stay lyrical, relevant, and talent-based. I admire the skills of the DJ, the skills of the breakdancer, the skills of the graffiti artist, the skills of the MC. When I hear artists saying, "Yo, I just want to get the paper," that pisses me off. When you say you don't really give a shit, and you just want to get on the radio, then you're pop to me. And pop has always been my enemy.

Frankly, I don't feel the fire anymore from the youth. I miss my era when motherfuckers were fighting for shit, spitting fire in their lyrics. When I went in on little homey, did I come off like a grumpy middle-aged dude? Probably. But so what? I'll own that shit. I'm Ice-T—one of them old thug motherfuckers that'll take your head off.

Don't get me wrong. I listen to *all* the new music. And there are intelligent cats doing it today. I like Young Jeezy and Lupe Fiasco and T.I. Lil' Wayne—when he wants to, when he ain't bullshittin'—can rap his ass off. And you've got cats like Jay-Z that are superskilled. Jay-Z is a jewel. One of the most dope rappers ever. I know Jay; I've seen him get busy in the booth, he doesn't even write shit down. Jay is just rap-gifted.

Eminem proved he's a master lyricist and promoter—and his last record went gold in two days. To me, that proves there's hope in the world. Even though Em did a few pop records to get on the radio and cement that fan base—he gets a pass for that. I always give Em mad love; right when he was coming out, he gave an interview talking about influences, and he said, "The very first rap record I ever heard was 'Reckless' by Ice-T." That's the electro-beat battling track I did with Dave Storrs and Chris "The Glove" Taylor, and it shows Eminem's hip-hop knowledge runs deep.

Drake is the man-of-the-moment. I won't front; the kid has talent. But Drake right now is ruling in a land where there's not that many great people. It's like Ali. We wouldn't recognize Ali's greatness if we hadn't seen him fight wars with other great heavyweights like Frazier, Foreman, Norton, Chuvalo. In every arena, in every era, you're defined by your comp edition. I hear people already trying to compare Drake to Jay-Z. My answer is: Okay, let's talk in *ten years*. After *ten albums*. But not on dude's first record. That just sounds stupid. There's a formula to reach a certain exalted status and be considered a G in our game: performance and consistency over time. Everybody's riding Drake. But in my book, right now Ludacris is the most dangerous spitter in the game.

I WAS BLESSED to come up during the Golden Age of Hip-Hop. I'm not claiming I'm one of the artists that's at the *top* of the list, but I was *there.* I ask people all the time, "Name the last *important* hip-hop album. Name the last *great* rapper." If they have any in-depth knowledge of hip-hop, they invariably reach back to artists from that golden era.

When I was in the studio in '85, '86, '87, I knew that Kane, KRS-One, Public Enemy, Eric B and Rakim were all in the studio at the same exact time, so I felt I was in a pressure cooker. The level of the game was at an all-time high. I couldn't put out lame bullshit.

The dudes I first met in New York: Grandmaster Caz, Grandmaster Flash—think on that: their very names got "master" in them. When you get to that point where you've mastered it, then you can teach it. These cats are not a joke. These cats are not a game.

In my day, one of the reasons that the talent pool in hip-hop was so deep was because there was a defined rite of passage. You used to have to work your way up to the mic. Now kids are just getting the mic because they get a record deal, and then they do their very first stage show.

No matter how much I talk about the Golden Age, people don't understand it. Because a lot of people who are coming up just weren't there. They don't understand Big Daddy Kane. They don't understand Rakim. They don't even know who KRS-One is or the impact that Public Enemy had on the world.

I kept saying it over and over in interviews in magazines and on TV. I kept talking about it in lectures. I got sick of repeating it. And after I got into it with Soulja Boy, I realized I couldn't convince these young cats with my words alone.

Show and prove. It's one of the things we say in the street. Don't tell me you're my friend. *Show* it. *Prove* it.

After the Soulja Boy situation, I was sitting home and thinking about the best way I could express my love for hip-hop, the best way I could show and prove. Then it hit me: I should make a documentary.

Actually, I got motivated after I had a cameo in Chris Rock's documentary, *Good Hair.* That was such a fun movie, it was shot so easily—he got me in one quick session. Truth be told, I didn't even *know* I was in the movie, until I heard about it coming out and me and Coco went to the New York premiere. I loved the way Chris shot that joint. Everyone carries digital cameras around now, I said. I can shoot a movie myself, guerilla style. I'll just interview all the rappers that I feel mean something. I went though my Rolodex and found out I knew every-fucking-body. I called them up and said, "Yo, I got twelve questions I wanna ask you."

The documentary follows my life, coming from L.A., wanting to be a rapper, meeting the cats in New York, then watching hip-hop go back to L.A. I talk to Ice Cube and groups from out West.

The movie is not about the money, the girls, the cars—none of that. I feel it's the definitive movie about the art form. It takes the best hip-hop artists of all time and asks them: How are you motivated and inspired? What are the techniques and the craft that go into making a great rhyme? How do we as rappers judge other rappers? Not the fans—the fans will jump on whoever's got the hottest record on the radio. Who do we—hip-hop artists—consider great?

The film breaks down the distinction between biting and being inspired by someone. Nobody's mad at inspiration. People are mad at biting—taking someone's shit and not giving credit. When I was coming up, for me not to give credit to King Sun or Schoolly D would be biting; but I always give those cats props for the rhymes that inspired me to write "6 in the Mornin'" and "Colors."

A lot of people bit off me over the years. I got a lyric that goes, "Motherfuckers are stealing shit I haven't even made up yet."

If there's any one thing I take pride in—as far as helping this hip-hop game to grow into the empire it is today—it's the number of firsts. I was the first L.A. rapper respected in New York. First rapper to drop that street language—*bitch, ho, nigga.* First to bring back the black heavy metal band in our generation. First rapper to write a book when I dropped my collection of essays, *The Ice Opinion,* in '92. First rapper to start acting in films. First rapper to land a role on a network television series.

But I always liked to switch up my game, get out of my comfort zone. Again, like Chuck D said, I'm the guy to jeopardize my entire career just to stay awake.

And I'm still looking to make some more firsts. I hope *The Art of Rap* will be seen as the definitive film about lyricism. It's going to show the world the passion we have for the music. And hopefully, if I'm lucky, the film will help reformat the game.

Frankly, I think my generation of hip-hop is like fine art. But if you don't understand fine art, you can't go see Picasso and Van Gogh—you won't get it. You need to know their stories. Once you understand Van Gogh cutting his ear off—his suffering, his loneliness, his heightened sense of reality—then you look at his paintings and *feel* them. You need to understand the Renaissance, Impressionism, Expressionism, all these schools of art, before you dive headfirst into the museum.

I don't know if it's possible to reformat the hip-hop game. I don't know if it's possible to educate a young generation about the pantheon of greats. Maybe I'm overly optimistic about *The Art of Rap.* If the documentary just stands up as a classic film about old-school rappers, so be it. I can live with that.

I'LL ALWAYS BE the kind of dude who speaks his mind. Fuck stepping on toes. I call it like I see it. But don't mistake that outspokenness for someone who likes initiating beefs. I've seen enough real violence in my life to know that it's nothing to be flippant about. In fact, if there's one thing the name Ice-T has stood for, both in the hip-hop game and in the street, it's been as a peacemaker.

Check this—in my era of hip-hop, dudes earned their stripes by battling. That was part of the art of rap: coming off the dome with some creative, cutting, spontaneous dis. Those legendary live battles between LL and Kool Moe Dee. And on wax between MC Shan and KRS-One. Niggas used to talk mad shit in lyrics; but niggas wasn't shooting each other over it. In fact, go back to a lot of those original rap battles—half the time the two "warring" crews would do stage shows together to promote their battle records.

But then the hip-hop game started to get more mixed up with the gangster world, back in the mid-to-late 1990s. Brothers who were not O.G.s—maybe they were small-time street cats making exaggerated claims in their records—started to bring the heavy-hitters and murderers from their old neighborhoods into their entourages. And these gangsters were beginning to see hip-hop as a legit hustle that they could muscle into—a lot safer than trying to beat the Feds at the drug game.

When that so-called East Coast vs. West Coast war broke out, the situation was troubling for me on a lot of levels. Because I was the first artist to rep the West who'd come out and built with the best of the New York cats. Because I'd been down with the Zulu Nation and created my own Rhyme Syndicate, telling the hip-hop community: Let's all do this. Let's all get paid. The pie is big enough—all of us can eat.

Even though it's common to see it still written up as such, there *never* was an East Coast vs. West Coast war. I never had a beef with the East Coast. It was just a hyped-up beef between two companies, Bad Boy and Death Row, between Puffy and Suge. But Suge never represented all of us on the West, and Puffy never represented all of the East.

Long before the shit started getting violent, when it was still basically a war of words on wax and in the hip-hop magazines, I was asked about it in an interview.

"I wish they would just squash it," I said. "Because they got power. And if they connect, it's on; we'll have a real black hip-hop power base. If they connected, maybe they could be the basis of a new Motown-like label for hip-hop. How could a kid from Compton dislike a kid from Brooklyn? They don't even know each other!"

But the situation was already too heated. And I was probably too idealistic in thinking that Suge and Puffy could shake hands, link their two ventures and start building an even bigger empire together.

'PAC AND I WERE CLOSE FRIENDS. I've known 'Pac since he was carrying record crates, down with Digital Underground. I got to work with 'Pac on "Last Words," which was a track with 'Pac, Cube, and me on the *2Pacalypse Now* album.

Roseanne Barr used to have a sketch-comedy show on FOX called

Saturday Night Special. 'Pac and I guest-hosted the show one night. We didn't have any idea what we were going to do, if we were going to rap or act or whatever.

For one of the skits we sang "You Don't Bring Me Flowers." It was a crazy-ass idea, and neither one of us would have done it *alone.* But because both of us were there, and because we had a lot of mutual respect, we said, "Okay, let's go for the joke." I wasn't worried about looking stupid, 'cause 'Pac was in it. He wasn't worried about looking stupid cause Ice was in it.

'Pac was cracking up the whole time, but I would not smile. I was singing my ass off, wearing a fedora and shades. I was trying to be the consummate professional and do it the way they wrote it.

That was a great moment, and it's the way I like to remember 'Pac. That was a side of him a lot of people didn't get to see. I knew it. Tupac was a great guy, hilarious—a fun cat. I know the flip side of almost all these hard-as-hell rappers. There's a flip side to a lot of folks. You can't judge any of us entertainers by our stage personas. People meet me today and they are scared as shit. They don't know I tell jokes and laugh just like any other normal cat.

'Pac came to me when he was just starting to beef with Biggie. He was on some wild shit. Riled up beyond words. He played me his record "Hit 'Em Up" in my studio. I think I was one of the first people to hear it. Right off the bat, he was coming at Big so *hard:* "That's why I fucked your bitch, you fat muthafucka . . ."

When a dude comes and plays you a record he hasn't even released, you're supposed to be happy, congratulating him, giving him a pound. But I was, like, "Uhhh . . . this is gonna cause a *problem . . .* Homey, this is gonna spiral into something bigger, you know?"

I was older and I told him, straight up: Why don't you go knock on Biggie's door and handle it? Just go figure this shit out man-to-man. Why you writing *records?*

He didn't want to hear it. He was hotheaded at the time. His group, the Outlawz, was with him in the room, and they were all buck wild and co-signing the drama. Tupac actually got kind of angry that I wouldn't ride with him. You know, I was a West Coast O.G., so I was supposed to ride with him on that beef.

He was pissed, but he respected the big homey. He felt like I should have been more amped up about shit.

But I was looking at the big picture, and it turned out to be fatal.

I do that all the time. Whenever there's conflict, I try to think through the consequences three or four steps ahead, like in chess. Honestly, I didn't expect the final result to be *that* tragic—two of our best young talents murdered while in their prime. But once I heard that track "Hit 'Em Up," I knew it wasn't going to end well.

THE MOOD IN THE STREET was so ugly, so hopeless, and dudes were scared there would be retaliation and escalation. I saw my role as stepping into the breach as a G, and acting as a mediator.

When Biggie was shot in L.A., I immediately called into Hot 97 in New York, offering my condolences to Biggie's family. I reminded the listeners that I'd always been one of the artists who worked with cats from both coasts, from New York and Cali. And I wasn't about to let the media distort shit, to blow up this personal rivalry, essentially a beef between two record labels, into some kind of East Coast vs. West Coast war. I got on the radio and said, "Yo, let's not start this rumor that East and West Coast got beef. I *love* Biggie and I know a gang of people in L.A. that love Biggie."

IT STILL HURTS ME that Big was murdered in L.A. You can't come from Los Angeles and not have the daily violence, the unsolved drive-by shootings, and the intergenerational gang situation weigh heavily on you. The thing of it is, fuck the rap music, as a person you're going to have certain things that matter to you. No bullshit: I can't count the number of my friends who got killed out in the street. I once dropped a rhyme that said:

> **I don't hate white people**
> **That's a well-known fact**
> **'Cause all of my homeys**
> **Got killed by blacks**

My career is so intrinsically tied to gangbanging; the songs I've made, the life I've depicted. As artists and celebrities, people are always urging us to "give back." What's the best way for me to give back? That was a question I ruminated over in my mind for a long time.

IN THE WAKE of the Rodney King verdicts, after the riots that tore L.A. apart in 1992, an unprecedented truce was called between long-warring gangs. Understand: I had *nothing* to do with setting the gang truce off. The gang truce jumped off between Imperial Courts and the Bounty Hunters, two projects right next door to each other in Watts. They've been lifetime enemies, and in the aftermath of the riots, they decided to forge a truce.

It was an organic thing; it couldn't have come from any outsiders. The Bounty Hunters and Imperial Courts shot callers had to initiate it. The truce was groundbreaking. That energy just rippled like after-shocks throughout the city. Dudes all around the city started talking about a peace treaty: "Cuz or Blood, it don't matter, yo. We gotta stop this murder and insanity."

The impetus came from all the first-generation gang members. Now, a first generation gang member would be my age—at most, a few years older. The thing about gangbanging is, it's all good when you're a kid, because you ain't thinking about the consequences or ramifications of all the dirt you're doing.

But when you have children and they become teenagers, then you start to see your kids cycling back into it. You watch that happening—powerless—and that's when it starts to hurt you.

We've now passed the second generation and are onto a third generation. And a lot of the first-generation gangbangers—the O.G.s—are coming home after long bids. A lot of them have had a change of heart; they've realized that the whole gang culture is negative, something they'd like to stop. Actually, at the O.G. level—across L.A.—most of the brothers do want peace.

The problem is getting that message down to the youngsters. The youngsters want reputations like the O.G.s got. They want the respect the O.G.s got. And as I said, gangbanging is fundamentally based on murder. How you going to tell some young brother to forgive another gangster who killed his uncle or his best friend or his father? How you going to tell him to sit down and make a truce with guys he's sworn to take vengeance against?

These young brothers are in it for life. Gangbanging ain't like a club that you can leave whenever you want. This is some real blood-war shit.

When the truce of '92 jumped off, I connected with one of my boys named Malik Spellman. He asked me to go down into Watts with him. I'm not from Watts, but I was well received. The brothers in Watts gave me love, and I connected to the gangsters down there. A brother named Tony Bogard from the Imperial Courts. A brother named Ty Stick out of the Bounty Hunters. We made a song and video called "Gotta Lotta Love." The video was shot at the start of the truce. In the lyrics, I just threw my excitement out there:

> I never thought I'd live to see us chill
> Crips and Bloods holdin' hands—the shit is ill
> But I love it, I can't help it
> Too much death on the streets, and we dealt it
> Van Ness Boys, The Hoovers, The 60s
> Bounty Hunters, Eight-Treys, all coolin' out, G
> I pray the shit'll never stop
> You used to see the wrong colors, and the gats went pop-pop
> But now the kids got a chance to live
> And the O.G.s got something to give
> That's love, black-on-black, that's how they made it
> And if any busters flip, they get faded
> L.A. is where I'm speakin' of
> Peace to all the gangsters, cause I gotta lotta love

A lot of other rappers were uncomfortable having their faces so closely associated with the gangs. But everyone knows my get-down; I honestly have no fear. Of course, I'm afraid of disease and shit like that, but I'm not afraid of confrontations with people. My attitude going into neighborhoods that were foreign to me—the Imperial Courts and Bounty Hunters turf—was: Okay, I know you're legit tough guys. But what are you gonna do? You gonna rob me? Here's my watch. You gonna kill me? For what? Did I do something to you? You gonna kill me just because you're jealous? See, if I didn't give you any reason to kill me, then why should I have fear?

It only takes six ounces of pressure. Any thirteen-year-old can kill you.

If I'm out there doing dirt, if I'm committing crimes, if I'm crossing other individuals, then maybe I have reason to live in fear. But I'm not doing that anymore. And I haven't lived like that in years.

So I told my man Malik: "Fuck it, let's do this. Let's go to the 'hood."

I was at as many meetings as I could be. Snoop Dogg got down with us, too, and as the peace treaty started to grow, me and Snoop became an integral part of—at least the public face of—the truce in L.A.

The high-water mark was this one massive gang summit at the Best Western on Century Boulevard. That meet was unprecedented: Gang representatives from all 'hoods were there. All the biggest shot callers, all the baddest Bloods and Crips—the ones not behind bars—who controlled the projects and streets. When it came my time to speak, I got up in front and told them that the answers were economic—we could police our own neighborhoods, but we needed help to create jobs and opportunities for the kids before they were already initiated into the gang life.

"Dig, ain't no way you gonna win a gang war," I said. "Y'all are gonna end up dead or in the penitentiary for life. Why we doing it then if there ain't *never* gonna be a winner?"

FAST-FORWARD. The truce is dead. Seventeen long years have passed. Gang warfare rules the streets again. Murder and retaliation every-fucking-day. The gang violence in L.A. is more entrenched than ever before.

If you're an outsider, you have to look at L.A. like it's a checkerboard. Take the aerial view: Every single one of those squares has its own different gang war going on within it. Not Crips–Bloods. These wars are way more specific: It's the 40s against the 40 Avalons. It's the Mansfields vs. the Playboy Gangsters. These are all Crips sets. The bloodshed happens within about eight square blocks.

Bloods fight each other, too. It's just whoever your closest neighbor is and who the fuck you've got a problem with. Then you got thousands and thousands of Mexican gangsters and they go to war with each other constantly.

I had done some work with the TV series *Gangland,* which airs on the History Channel and tries to give insight into America's gangs—black, white, Asian, and Latino. In fact, I'm the voiceover that comes on right at the start. No disrespect to *Gangland* but I feel like it tends to glamorize the violence. It gives the 'bangers the chance to yell and posture. At the end the gangster is usually saying, "Don't do what I did" or "Damn, I threw the best years of my life away for nothing." But for me, it doesn't really humanize the gang member.

Sitting around the crib, I had one of my brainstorms: "Let's do a show where we go in and try to catch the warring gang factions and get them to sit down together. I've even got the perfect title. We'll call it *The Peacemaker.*"

Everyone thought I was nuts.

"Ice, how could you do this? They're at war!"

"Dig," I said, "My man Malik, this is what he does. This is his specialty. He's a 'gang interventionist.'"

We pitched the concept to Asylum Entertainment and they liked it. Gave us a little budget. Before you knew it we were out in the streets filming the first episodes of *The Peacemaker,* which we developed and sold to the A&E network.

The first gangs we shot were the 40s and 40 Avalons. That's a war that's been going on for twenty years. Malik was able to reach out to O.G.s and get them to sit down for a meeting.

We don't set any terms or any agenda. When they have the meeting, it doesn't have to come off positive, but at least it's a conversation. This is often the first time these enemies have seen one another and not drawn weapons.

After getting the 40s to sit down with the 40 Avalons we did an episode with P. J. Watts and Mona Park. Then we did Mansfield Crips and Playboy Gangster Crips. *The Peacemaker* is unlike any documentary television that's come before: It's dramatic, dynamic, hardcore. The most difficult part of the show is the sheer volatility; there's a very good chance somebody might get shot on camera.

A&E was a bit freaked when I told them that.

"Somebody might get *shot?*" one of the producers asked.

"Yeah," I said. "We in the 'hood, man! Niggas is bangin'. Hell yeah, somebody might get shot."

To A&E's credit, they didn't get cold feet. They picked us up, bought the first five episodes. Said if the first five do well, they'll greenlight us to make another twenty.

I'm executive producer, and it's a labor of love for me. There's no real money being made on the show. But I'm passionate about it.

For me, this puts the *real* in reality TV. This ain't no *Survivor, Amazing Race,* or *Jersey Shore.* This is real to the point where the guys we are interviewing are armed. At any minute, they could pull out and kill the cameraman. During our show, people are getting shot on each side of the borderline.

It's war correspondence. It's just war correspondence in the heart of the City of Angels.

What the show illustrates is that these gangbangers are not monsters. It humanizes the gangster rather than showing kids getting all *rah-rah-rah,* showing their guns, throwing up their set and mean-mugging for the camera. You see their children, you see their parents; you get a sense of the depth of their anger and *why* they're so angry.

In the Mansfield Crips episode, we came in right after this guy's wife and baby had been shot. Imagine that: Wife and the baby are fresh homicide victims. We're coming in and telling the dude, "Do not retaliate."

And every show starts like that, with a murder. It's intense. Fuck *Jersey Shore*—this is the realest shit that's ever been on television.

PART EIGHT

TOO FAMOUS TO STEAL

"MY LIFE IS VIOLENT
BUT VIOLENT IS LIFE
PEACE IS A DREAM
REALITY IS A KNIFE."
—"COLORS"

16.

ONCE YOU'VE TESTED the fire, you become very comfortable with the calm. These days, I'm in a quiet zone. I prefer staying in the crib, eating at my own table, chilling with my wife. The only blood and mayhem comes when I'm playing Xbox. *Call of Duty. Red Dead Redemption.* I can play that shit all day long. I love gaming so much. Last year I was even asked to voice the character Griffin in this dope-ass third-person shooter game called *Gears of War 3.*

Some actors can't take a day out of the limelight. I can hole up in the crib with Coco for two weeks. Like we say: *Low-profile is better than no profile. And slow motion is better than no motion.*

At the end of the day, we're all trying to find some peace. It's easier to find it if you've seen the world, explored every avenue that's open to you. "Okay, I've seen it, I found it, now I can relax." It's harder when you haven't. A lot of folks, as U2 says it, still haven't found what they're looking for. They never achieved what they wanted in life, so they remain on edge, always searching.

In my view, that's why a lot of successful people commit suicide. Because when they finally make it big, get to this supposed finish line of fame and fortune, they look around and think: This is it? This is what I've been working for all these years? Fuck.

Then they slip into depression.

And that depression takes them out.

I've never made it to Michael Jackson or Bill Gates levels, but I've seen a certain degree of success. I know what it's like in the fame-and-fortune lane. Me and Coco were in Las Vegas recently and we got to reflecting about our lives. Okay, we're eating at the best restaurants. We're staying in a beautiful suite at the finest hotel. We're driving a hell of a nice car. How much more can you do? Once you're on a yacht, you're on the same damn ocean as everybody else. Is there anything that we *ought* to do that we're unable to do? Outside of wasting money on jewelry you really don't need or designer clothes you're never going to wear but once? Is there something more? Is there another level?

And we came to the conclusion that there really is no other level. The only other level is to do it like we're doing it, but take as many people as possible with you for that ride. You can't count the number of dudes—Mike Tyson's just one—who damn near went broke trying to take an entourage of fifty motherfuckers along for the ride.

In the music business, and especially in the hip-hop game, everybody's competing on a materialistic level. Everybody's trying to do it. But that's pretty straightforward. Once you get into the world of the superwealthy, it's not about how much money you make or how many mansions you have; it's about how much money you're giving away—how many tens of millions you're allocating to charities, museums, hospitals.

Sure, you can decide you want to play that debutante game, you want to play the De Beers and Van Cleef & Arpels game, and your wife has to have estate jewels and wear next season's clothes off the runways of Milan and Paris every day. That's like an infinite spiral staircase to me. You'll keep ascending but never reach the fucking top.

And there's a point where you're living large and you say, "Damn. Am I having a good time or am I not?" My view is: If you're caked-out and still asking yourself if you're having a good time—homey, you ain't.

And the fame side? Of course, you get to a level of notoriety—like Michael Jackson at the end—where it's too much. It's a noxious bubble. He was one of the most famous and gifted entertainers in the history of the world, but who the fuck would want to be trapped living in that sad world M.J. was in at the end of his life? '

If I could press cruise control on my career right now, I'd be happy for the rest of my life. I make enough money. I've got fame. I've got respect. Nobody's life is perfect. You have to accept that. Once you come to terms with the fact that there is no perfection of life, then you can be happy. I feel that true wisdom is accepting that the trauma, disruption, uneasiness—that's just part of life. Everybody's going to have that till they die. And if you're lucky enough to get your life feeling almost perfect, one of your friends' lives is going to be so fucked-up, or one of your relative's lives is going to be so fucked-up, that their drama is going to invade your space. The trick is how to deal with that unhappiness, to compartmentalize the anxiety, and still find happiness at the same time.

I've got news for you: If you feel that you can't find happiness unless you're 100 percent absolutely carefree and blissful, then I'm sorry, man, but you're going to be a miserable, depressed person forever.

And I know the feeling. Sure, I've been down, been depressed before. I believe depression is all a matter of perspective. As Americans, I think that's the main thing we lack: a global outlook. I tell people all the time: "Yo, if you think you're really depressed, I need to take you to some places in Africa or the Middle East. I think I need to take you to Somalia or Sudan or Soweto. So you can get an understanding of human suffering. So you can get some perspective, partner."

I know—there's true clinical depression, a chemical imbalance in the brain that often needs medication and therapy to straighten out. But there's an aspect of depression, too, that I believe is simply a form of isolation. When you really get deep into depression, your mind is so warped that you honestly feel you're the only person on earth going through this pain. I've read that, statistically, the most unhappy place is the Upper East Side in Manhattan; the country's richest zip code has the highest percentage of people on antidepressants and antianxiety meds. Think about that. That's proof that money does not buy happiness.

If you're a guy who's done all right in life, you've hit the age of forty or fifty and looked around you: You're living the American dream, you've got a good wife and kids, a good home, a good job—shit, you should be feeling *great* about yourself, because you done *did* it, man! But too many of us get to that point and actually feel like shit. Feel hopeless and empty.

Sometimes I use what I call a "gym" philosophy. Everybody knows that feeling of hitting the gym to work out, you look over to the right, see somebody in way better shape—that makes you feel like shit. But then you look to your left, you see somebody who would *die* to be in your shape. Again—it's a matter of perspective.

You notice that the most balanced and secure folks stop comparing themselves to other people, try to contain that envy, and find happiness in smaller things. Like the old-timers used to say: best to count your blessings.

People tell me all the time, "Oh Ice, you show up to work. You're so easygoing. You're so calm."

I have *real* reference points. My friends call me from Pelican Bay, the supermax state prison in Crescent City, California. I got friends doing the kind of time that only ends with them leaving the pen in a wheelchair or a wooden box. Man, I *know* what my options are! I can't go back to the streets. I can't go back to them old days.

As an adult—if you've got any sense—you don't want to go to the pen. I've spent a few nights in jail. Everybody in there acting hard. Everybody lying about what they did. I just felt like, "Yo, we in here because we stupid. Everybody trying to act like they ain't stupid. But stupidity is the only reason we got caught."

Don't get me wrong, I got friends that can do time standing on their heads. Dudes will call me straight after sentencing. "They gave me five, Ice. I'll be right back." *What?* Five *years?* I can't do five minutes, homey.

About seven or eight years ago, I was out in L.A., sitting around with a bunch of my friends. This is what I call my crime group—a bunch of the old guys I used to get down with. This was the start of the dialogue: *Yo, there would be no sense going on a lick unless it's a retirement lick.* It's different from when you're a kid and your train of thought is, *Man, all I need is ten thousand dollars and I could buy this car.* The problem for our crew—it was five of us sitting around—in order to go on a retirement lick, the score would have to be in the ballpark of $10 million.

Because there's no way you can retire with $1 million these days. Every one of us would want at least $2 million apiece and in order to do a $10 million lick, people are going to *die.* And if something like that happens, you're on the run for the rest of your life.

That's just no longer an option. We've all got kids. We've all got families. We can't live on the run. Back in the day, going on the lam was okay by me. It was almost fun. If shit got hot in L.A., cool, I was a one-man operation. I could hide. I could disappear. Lay low in Oregon. Or jet back to Hawaii. I could get out of town for three months if I needed to. I can't do that shit now.

Actually, sometimes I still feel I'm living on the run. I'm still ducking and dodging. Bouncing all over the country. I tell people that the only difference is, these days, I'm staying in the best hotels.

I'LL NEVER FORGET THE DAY—the exact moment—when I knew that I was out of the game. I had an experience in Los Angles that told me I was finished—done with breaking the law. It's ironic, because it wasn't even a big lick. It was some little bullshit. I wanted a part for my Porsche. This was just early in my recording career, I had a few records out, the name Ice-T was starting to ring a few bells. I wasn't doing the acting thing yet.

We had a Porsche shop that we normally gave our business to, but for some fucking reason, when I woke up that morning, I did not want to pay for the part I needed to fix my convertible roof mechanism. The part was only worth about five hundred bucks, but I wanted to *steal* it. Some of my friends had stolen a Porsche—not the same make or model as mine, but I knew the part would fit.

They were supposed to bring me the convertible part, and I kept bugging them about it. Finally, I was frustrated. So once again Mr. Ice went gung ho on their asses: "Where's that muthafuckin' car? You muthafuckas can't steal. Where's that fuckin' stolen car?"

They told me the address and I went on this solo mission to go get this part for my Porsche. The stolen car was parked in the structure of an apartment building. It was well hidden; had a canvas car cover over it. I got the ratchet in my waistband and I was focused. I had a point to prove to my partners: *Yo, I'm'a show you muthafuckas—you peons—this is how a real fuckin' criminal steals!*

I walked to the apartment building. Made a beeline straight for the Porsche, then peeled off the canvas tarp. I get my ratchet out, I'm standing inside the Porsche, about to steal the part, and suddenly I hear screaming. I whirl around and at least ten kids from the apartment building above have spotted me. They shouted so fucking loud, and a few are now streaming out of this door, running toward me.

For a second I thought they were calling for the police to bust my ass. But no—as they ran closer I saw the pieces of paper and pens. They were asking for autographs.

"Ice-T! Ice-T!"

"Yo, it's Ice-T! Yo, sign this, Ice!"

In the heat of my criminal-mindedness, I'd completely forgotten that I even *was* Ice-T. I was just back into that zone where I was a bad guy, a straight-up hustler.

My face was well-enough known that somebody from one of those windows above me had spotted me lifting the tarp just as I pulled out my ratchet.

Now I'm sitting in this Porsche half-stealing this part—stone-cold busted, because I got the ratchet in my hand—and I have to put on this big cheesy smile.

"Hey! What's up, lil' homey? Y'all want autographs?"

Before I could even blink, a bunch of their parents are running outside. And they all want autographs, too. So now I end up signing autographs for fifteen minutes, managed to duck any photographs. Luckily, this was the age before digital cameras and cellphone cameras.

Nobody even looked at me askance. It appeared so innocent. All the residents of the building naturally assumed it was my own Porsche I'd parked there for some fucking reason. So that's when I realized, with a little bit of sadness: Damn! I can't do this anymore. I'm too famous to steal.

I HAD A SITUATION not that long ago—a serious altercation with some people out here in New York. I can't get too specific about where or when, but the situation got violent. When we left the building there were people laid out. Nobody died, fortunately. But it was some serious shit. When I got home I was real sullen and contemplative for hours.

Damn, Ice. That was your whole career right there. You're out here acting on instinct—but in the heat of the moment, did you even think about the twenty-five years of busting your ass? Man, you can't do this anymore.

There's a basic street law: talk shit, get punched in the face. Everybody knows that law. Different folks have different lines. And my line is *way* to the left. I'm the kind of dude that if I accidentally step on your shoes and you say, "Hey! What the hell?" I'll not only apologize, I'll wipe them off for you. "My bad, money, my bad." But if apologizing to you is not enough, if you still want to talk shit, then I could flip a switch and go to a very bad place. You dig?

So this particular guy got out of pocket, crossed that line, and I had to flip the switch. It got real ugly, real fast. . . .

After that I sat at my house for a couple days, waiting it out. Waiting for the cops to come. But they never came. Still, it was a moment of reckoning. I had to talk to my wife. I had to talk to everybody in my crew.

I said, "Yo, I can't even go *outdoors* if this type of stuff is going to happen. I have to contain myself. I need everybody's help. You know how I get down. Let's avoid this." And so every day, since that altercation, I've just become much, much, much more passive. From time to time I still get angry, of course, but I've just learned how to contain it. It's a tough psychological trick. You have to learn to channel the anger into something positive. For me it's not a matter of choice. Certain people have to learn how to channel their rage or they're just going to end up locked up.

THAT'S THE DOUBLE-EDGED SWORD. At the end of the day, looking back on my career, I believe that whatever respect I've got comes from the fact that the people that I was involved with in the life—hustlers, pimps, and killers—know that I was an active person in the game. I actively did everything I rhymed about. That's why I've gone twenty-five years doing this shit. That's the *only* way you go twenty-five years rapping autobiographically and never have your credibility challenged.

You've never heard anybody come out and say, "Man, Ice-T's a fake. Ice-T didn't do this. Ice-T didn't do that." As far-fetched as I can make things sound, whenever I go someplace in Los Angeles or travel around the country, cats will tell a story exactly the same way that I tell it—not one single detail changed or exaggerated.

I had a record where I said:

> **My life's been a great story in the ultimate war**
> **Should I ill or do right? Make peace or go raw?**
> **I can't explain the true penalties of fame and the wealth**
> **Tell me who can I trust? I can't trust myself**
> **The devil got me thinking 'bout them ill moves**
> **Every damn kid on the street, they got something to prove**
> **Push a bullet through my heart, why not? That's a start**
> **They could pump their reps quicker, kill a well-known nigga . . .**

I know what it would be like for a youngster to kill me—to murder a "well-known nigga." I know exactly what he's thinking: *Fuck a old dude. Think I give a fuck? Ain't nothin', cuz.*

That's one of my skills as a writer, being able to flip my brain back to being twenty-one years old. Understanding that ruthless, reckless mentality is what keeps me safe. As they age, people tend to lose that mental agility. I use it all the time in making music.

Most people hear an unexpected knock on the door—they picture a friend of theirs, a neighbor, maybe a deliveryman. I *always* see the fucking ski masks. I see the motherfuckers storming into my world on some ready-to-die shit. That's just the dark, twisted imagery I always have in my mind.

———————————

FUNNY STORY about Quentin Tarantino. I loved *Reservoir Dogs* and *Pulp Fiction*—all Quentin's movies, and especially his scripts, are off-the-chain. So I went to Tarantino one day, told him that I wanted some help writing a screenplay.

"Quentin," I said, "I've got a movie idea and I wanted to get your advice—" He cut me off.

"Dude," he said. "Where do you think I get all *my* ideas from? From your music! You don't need any help from *me* writing anything."

FOR ALL THE DIRT I did, I'm the kind of dude that would always try to learn something from the dark side of life, take away a lesson and then I'd put it in a record.

In my younger days, I saw myself as this guy running down a road—this hustling road—and yelling at everybody on my left and right: "Yo, you not gonna win! I'm the baddest at this shit!"

And then when I got to what I thought was the finish line, the end of that hustling road, I saw that there was a steep cliff. And all my friends who were hustling with me, they kept falling off that cliff.

Now I'm the guy who's spun around, running back up the road, yelling at folks:

"Don't do it! Ain't nothin' up there but a fuckin' cliff!"

All I see are smirks and slick glances. "Yo, you're a sucker!" and "Fuck you, Ice. I'm ten times smarter than you."

I understand them. I've been them. Some cats just ain't ready for the truth. They don't get it.

But they'll get it when they reach that cliff.

I can't convince everybody, but I look at this way: At least I'm *yelling*.

LOVE KEEPS YOU ALIVE in the game—not fear. Never fear. When you get to that certain level of O.G., no one's afraid of anybody. But if motherfuckers love you, you're straight.

Love's the reason I can connect with the brothers doing hard time. When I go into prison, see the homeys, I just humble myself. I sit there in the visiting room and listen to them. We chop it up for hours. That's who gives me the motivation to stay the course.

When you talk to the lifers in a joint like Sing Sing, they know it's too late for them. They've written their past, their present, and their future. It's a sealed book. But more than anything else, these guys doing life in prison want me to be a transmitter to the young kids. They're trying to give me the information that I can translate to a young buck *before* he goes to jail.

Crime is a macho brainwashing, a psychological warp where you begin to believe you're bigger than the rest of the world because you know how to break the law and get away with it. Sure, there's something sexy about being the outlaw. Once you buy into that and you're out to break the law, decide you can't work a square job, feel that you're something special, you're running head on into the machine that says, "Hold on. Nope. We gonna keep you in line."

Whatever slick shit you think you're doing on the street, you're good until the fucking Feds get you in their sights. When you're small-time, no one gives a fuck about you. Once they decide that you're big enough to warrant fifty or a hundred agents on you, dude, you're a *wrap*. I don't give a fuck who you are. Ain't nobody untouchable.

Like we always used to say when I was pulling jewelry licks: You raise the risk, you raise the profit. But also—you raise the risk, you raise the problem.

So when I talk to the kids in various juvenile facilities, I tell 'em. "Look at y'all. Y'all got caught, and you're still little petty punks. You're in juvie, a bunch of petty criminals. What makes you think you can be a *big-time* gangster, and you won't get caught again? You're already fucking up and you're in the first grade!"

Then I've got one question that usually wipes the smirks off their faces: "Do you know anyone who's over thirty that's *never* been to jail and *never* been caught?"

No one raises a hand.

"Think on that. Why would you get into a business when you know there's no way out? Listen, the smart hustlers are the ones who figure a legit hustle and take it to the bank. You can still keep your swagger, you can still be cool, you can still have all that fly shit—but don't get it twisted: We ain't in the day of Jesse James when you could rob banks and ride three hundred miles and nobody's going to chase you down. The cops got GPS tracking, helicopters, plus all them innocent bystanders with camera phones putting your ass on YouTube—a thousand technological advantages for the Feds and local cops to nail your ass.

The kids I'm talking to think they're real slick. But that's cool, too. I understand them because I was one of them. Bottom line, all criminals want to do is live that good life. They think they found a slicker route to the money.

"Yeah, you been online, homey? You seen the pictures of me with the Bentley Continental and Lamborghini Murcielago? Check this out. I came from nothing. I was homeless. My parents died when I was younger than you. I tried my luck at all the illegal shit that you guys are trying your luck at. But look how I'm doing in the legit world. And they said I couldn't do it."

Now you do have some sociopaths out there, people who are definitely hardcore violent or twisted people who get off on the sheer aggression. Some get off on the pleasure of domination, or inflicting pain. I never was that kind of guy. I never got off on being tough or aggressive. I loved the excitement of crossing the line. Also, I just thought I was slick.

Of course, living the life, I ran into some dangerous individuals. You gotta stay clear of them cats if you're not one of them Most of the cats in the street life keep a small circle of people they fuck with, because they really don't know how some outside dudes will get down. You don't know if they're psychopaths. You don't know what they gonna do under pressure. Notice how the Mob families keep it real tight— they've been burned by undercovers and snitches—but in the old days, they used to have it so they never allowed an unknown entity inside the circle.

You never know when you might brush into some cat ready to flip. Like Melle Mel said, "Don't push me 'cause I'm close to the edge." That's why I always lived by the credo, "I'm not out here to prove

I'm the toughest guy in the room. I just want to make it out of the room."

These kids in juvenile jails are tough. They can do their bids. It's a badge of honor to them. The frustrating thing about prison is that it's something you've got to take a lot of before you really understand the consequences. I've got friends that were in supermax prisons *twenty* years before I heard them crack, before I heard them change their tune. *Yo, man there's other things I can be doing.*

I got a global look at life around the time I nearly died in the car crash. I was thinking: Look I'm so slick, but I'm struggling with paper now and then. Meanwhile, all these so-called squares got nice houses, sending their kids to Spring Break, and ain't never thinking about the police. What the fuck's the matter with this picture?

It's really tough for young folks to understand consequences. And one thing I've learned, delaying consequences doesn't help. That's why I trip when I see these Hollywood folks, these starlets like Lindsay Lohan, getting locked up over bullshit like a DUI. I mean—what the fuck? What's the matter with these squares? I understand if you and me are bank robbers and we go to jail—if we're out here breaking the law, we're gangsters, bang-bangers, then getting knocked—that's an occupational hazard. Jail's part of our programming. If we get it, we get it. We're tough guys, right? But Lindsay, you are an *actress*! You got money. You got options. You don't even need to be *trying* to fuck with jail. Who the hell around you is giving you advice? Lindsay, do you really want to go in there and spend three months with some hard-ass jail bitches?

MY SCHEDULE IS SUPERTIGHT these days shooting *Special Victims Unit*—since the cancellation of the original *Law & Order, SVU* has assumed the mantle of NBC's flagship drama, coming off our twelfth season. I'm also recording new tracks, shooting more episodes of *The Peacemaker,* and putting together a bunch of other business deals. I'm always hustling. I never stop making moves. But like we always say, "The best hustle is the legit hustle."

Still, one aspect of my career I always make time for is traveling the country talking to young folks. I've been booked to speak at Harvard, Princeton, Stanford, UC Berkeley, as well as dozens of historically black colleges and universities.

As cool as it is to hit the college lecture circuit—who could have imagined that an ex-hustler from Crenshaw Boulevard would be spitting game to Ivy League students?—the most satisfying thing I can do with my time is talk to little kids. Sometimes it's organizations like the Boys and Girls Club of America. Sometimes it's at public elementary, junior, and high schools. Sometimes it's kids in group homes or juvenile facilities.

For a while at least, I try to stop being Ice-T, try to hit them with the advice of Tracy Marrow—lessons I picked up on my journey as an orphaned eleven-year-old who followed the criminal world's song before finding success in the entertainment industry.

I'm not naïve. When I talk to kids, I know damn well that if I was *broke* they wouldn't give a fuck what I have to say. But they see the success. They want to know how to be successful. That's the only reason people follow anybody, from preachers to politicians. It's in human nature to chase success. *He did it—how can I do it?*

When I talk to kids, I have to walk in with—metaphorically—my gold records and my movie and TV credits. With all my trappings of success. Only then can I zero in and catch their attention.

One thing I always stress to kids, one of the key lessons that drove me toward success, is "Don't be afraid to take a loss." You're guaranteed to miss 100 percent of the shots you don't take. You've got to be able to fail. As a dude, if every girl you talk to has to *like* you, you'll never hook up. You've got to work the averages. A girl gives you the brush-off—so what? Maybe she's having a bad day. Maybe she's got a better-looking boyfriend. Maybe you just look fucking nasty to her. Whatever, man.

Nobody wins 100 percent of the time. A lot of people stagnate in life because they're so afraid to lose. They use that fear as a crutch to not even try. Michael Jordan was the best I ever saw playing hoops and didn't hit 100 percent of his jump shots. Babe Ruth had his fair share of strikeouts. You gotta know that's part of the game. I'm in a career now—acting—where rejection hits you in the face every goddamn day. Like we say, "Charge that to the game."

As hustlers, we also used to say: "It ain't about the come up—it's about the comeback." Anybody can come up, but can they come *back*? That's where you get your stripes. If you take an L, you have to get your shit together, shake it off, and come back. The biggest winners in life are the cats best at absorbing losses. Once you know how to fail, only then you can get in the game.

Whenever I'm talking to kids—whether it's at elementary schools or Ivy League colleges—at the end of the day, I can't help but throw down a few intellectual challenges.

"Read everything you can get your hands on, absorb all the knowledge at your fingertips," I tell them. "Education is a beautiful thing. But remember, the most important thing to do is to *think*. Don't think the way I do or follow everything I say, because then it'll be just *one* of us thinking."

I tell them about Sergeant Donovan getting in my face and saying I was a loser who could never make it in the civilian world. I tell them that anger can be a great motivator if you channel it. How haters can drive you to success if you don't allow that hate or resentment to eat up your insides.

"That's the flip side of success; the haters out there will always try to fuck your head up," I say. "I'll be minding my own business, walking down the street, and some clown starts yelling: 'Yo, Ice! You ain't Will Smith!'"

You have to understand, if you're trying to achieve something positive in life, you must be prepared for the negative attention that will come your way. People waiting to see you fail. People happy to see you in handcuffs.

That's just part of the game.

No one hates *down*. They hate *up*.

Look, I've been taken down by the fucking *government,* and I'm still standing. One thing I've learned is that there is just no way that you're going to make everybody happy. Absolutely no way. So you just concern yourself with the people that you love, your intimate circle, and the people in the same intelligence bracket as you. And as long as you're getting the co-sign from them, you're straight. Fuck the haters. Best believe your real friends will pull your coat when you do something wrong. That's all you need to worry about.

Respect is built and gained in combat. So if success is what you want, prepare for war.

DAILY GAME

(OF LIFE)

1. AFTER ALL THE BULLSHIT I'VE BEEN THROUGH, IT IS AB-SOLUTELY *IMPOSSIBLE* FOR ME TO HAVE A BAD DAY. I SIM-PLY WILL NOT ALLOW IT.

2. AT SOME POINT, A STREET HUSTLER *MUST* ELEVATE HIS OR HER STREET HUSTLE TO SOMETHING LEGIT. IF NOT, PRISON OR DEATH IS GUARANTEED.

3. YOU DON'T WANNA GET RICH . . . AND DIE TRYING!

4. THE HUSTLER'S QUESTION IS: HOW BAD DO YOU WANT IT? THEN GO GET IT MOTHERFUCKER! GET OFF YOUR ASS . . . MOVE!

5. LIFE ISN'T ABOUT THE MATERIAL THINGS YOU OWN. (THERE'S NO LUGGAGE RACK ON A HEARSE.) IT'S ABOUT THE EXCEPTIONAL EXPERIENCES YOU HAVE.

6. EVERYDAY I WAKE UP, GO TO THE 'NET AND FIND SOME-THING NEGATIVE ABOUT ME THAT SOMEBODY'S SAYING. THEN I USE THAT AS MOTIVATION FOR THE DAY.

7. AS YOU GROW, THE GAME *YOU* PLAY GETS MORE AD-VANCED. NEVER LET MINOR LEAGUE PLAYERS PULL YOU BACK TO THEIR LEVEL.

8. THE ONLY WAY TO MAKE HISTORY IS TO START SOMETHING, SAVE SOMETHING, OR FUCK SOMETHING UP. I THINK I'VE DONE 'EM ALL.

9. THE MOST DANGEROUS PERSON ISN'T THE TOUGH GUY; IT'S THE PERSON WHO JUST WANTS TO BE LEFT ALONE— AND YOU'RE FUCKIN' WITH HIM.

10. LIFE IS FUCKED UP . . . GET A HELMET.

11. IT'S NOT HARD TO CONVINCE THE STREETS YOU'RE A GANGSTER. IT'S HARD TO CONVINCE THE FEDS YOU'RE NOT.

12. PEOPLE NEVER REMEMBER THE HUNDREDS OF TIMES YOU SAID "YES" TO THEM OR HELPED THEM OUT, BUT THEY ALWAYS REMEMBER THAT ONE TIME YOU SAID "NO."

13. IT'S NOT ABOUT BEING MAD AT *EVERYTHING;* IT'S ABOUT BEING *REALLY MAD* AT THE RIGHT THINGS.

14. THE KEY TO WINNING THE GAME: DON'T WORRY ABOUT *EVERYONE.* FIND OUT WHO'S ON *YOUR* SIDE AND ROLL WITH THEM!

15. WHEN YOU'RE PAID, A LOT OF BROKE PEOPLE WILL TALK SHIT ABOUT YOU—THAT'S ALL THEY HAVE.

16. DON'T JUST WATCH HOW YOUR FRIENDS TREAT YOU. NOTICE HOW THEY TREAT OTHERS. IF THEY TREAT OTHERS FUCKED UP, IT JUST MIGHT NOT BE YOUR TURN YET.

17. YOUNG PEOPLE THINK THEY KNOW EVERYTHING BECAUSE THEY DON'T REALIZE HOW *MUCH* THERE IS TO KNOW.

18. THINGS WILL ALWAYS GET BETTER. IF NOT, THE LAST TIME YOU WERE SICK AND THOUGHT YOU WERE DYING, YOU WOULD HAVE.

19. ALWAYS REFER TO COPS AS "OFFICER" WHEN SPEAKING TO THEM. THEY HAVE *RESPECT* ISSUES. GIVE 'EM THAT, AND YOU MIGHT SLIDE PAST 'EM.

20. STOP ASKIN' FOR SHIT AND GO AND GET SOMETHING!

21. A PLAYER DOESN'T LIE TO WOMEN; HIS LADIES ALL KNOW WHAT'S UP. IF YOU'RE LYING AND SNEAKING, YOU'RE NOT A PLAYER, YOU'RE A CHEATER.

22. IN THE GAME, SPECTATORS, COMMENTATORS, AND CRITICS DON'T GET THE TROPHIES—ONLY THE PLAYERS DO!

23. PEOPLE ALWAYS HATE UP. YOU NEVER THINK TWICE ABOUT SOMEONE BELOW YOU. IT'S THE PEOPLE ABOVE YOU WHO CREATE THE ENVY IN YOU.

24. IF I SEEM SQUARE TO YOU NOW IT'S BECAUSE I'VE BEEN THROUGH THE *WAR* AND HAVE LEARNED ITS LESSONS.

25. SOMETIMES WE CHOOSE TO REJECT GOOD ADVICE BECAUSE IT'S NOT WHAT WE WANT TO HEAR. REMEMBER, MEDICINE DOESN'T TASTE GOOD.

26. NO MAN CAN BE GREAT ALONE, NO MATTER WHAT HE THINKS. YOU'RE ONLY GREAT WHEN GOOD PEOPLE SPEAK OF YOU IN HIGH REGARD.

27. MONEY ALONE CANNOT MAKE YOU HAPPY. MONEY ONLY CREATES *OPTIONS.* HAPPINESS IS PSYCHOLOGICAL.

28. A THUG WILL HURT YOU BAD. A GANGSTER WILL *HAVE* YOU HURT BAD.

29. A NERD TALKS ABOUT IT. A GEEK CAN ACTUALLY DO IT.

30. I'VE FORGOTTEN MORE ABOUT THE GAME THAN MOST OF THESE CATS WILL EVER KNOW.

31. I'VE BEEN YOUR AGE, YOU'VE NEVER BEEN MINE—PAY AT-TENTION.

32. UP AT 5:00 AM AND OFF TO THE SET. YOU AIN'T HUSTLIN' UNLESS YOU'RE CATCHING A SWEAT.

33. IN BUSINESS, WHEN SOMEONE SAYS MAKING THE MONEY WILL BE *EASY,* GET OUT OF THE DEAL. THERE IS *NO WAY* TO MAKE EASY MONEY.

34. A RICH PERSON GOING BROKE IS FAR MORE SCANDALOUS THAN A POOR PERSON TRYING TO SURVIVE.

35. MEN WANT THREE WOMEN: 1) FREAK/PARTY GIRL; 2) HUSTLER/MONEY-GETTER; AND 3) WIFE/MOTHER. WE'LL EITHER FIND ONE THAT'S ALL THREE . . . OR HAVE THREE SEPARATE ONES.

36. OLD FRIENDS WILL PULL YOU BACK TOWARD YOUR OLD WAYS. UNFORTUNATELY, SOMETIMES YOU JUST GOT TO CUT THEM LOOSE TO MOVE FORWARD.

37. A BULLET WILL HIT YOU *BEFORE* YOU HEAR THE SOUND OF THE SHOT.

38. SLOW MOTION IS BETTER THAN NO MOTION, AND LOW PROFILE IS BETTER THAN NO PROFILE.

39. THE DIFFERENCE BETWEEN A HUSTLER AND A GAMBLER: GAMBLERS TAKE RISKS; HUSTLERS NEVER PLAY A GAME THEY CAN LOSE.

40. EVERY DAY SOMEONE ASKS ME WHERE I LEARNED HOW TO ACT. ANSWER: STANDING IN FRONT OF A *JUDGE* IN *COURT*.

41. SEX IS ONLY DIRTY . . . WHEN IT'S DONE RIGHT.

42. IF YOU SPENT HALF THE TIME ON YOURSELF THAT YOU SPEND SWEATING THE NEXT MAN, YOU MIGHT ACCOMPLISH SOMETHING WITH *YOUR* LIFE.

43. YOU'RE ONLY WASTING YOUR TIME TRYING TO TELL PEOPLE HOW FLY YOU ARE. IF IT'S *REAL* IT'S GONNA SHOW.

44. IT'S HARDER TO HIT A MOVING TARGET. PLAYERS KEEP IT MOVING.

45. NEVER CONFUSE POPULARITY WITH RESPECT.

46. IF EVERYONE YOU KNEW STOOD IN A ROOM AND THREW THEIR PROBLEMS IN THE AIR, I BET YOU'D REACH FOR *YOURS* ON THE WAY DOWN.

47. ALL A REAL PLAYER NEEDS TO WIN THE GAME IS HEALTH AND FREEDOM. WITH THAT, ANYTHING IS POSSIBLE.

48. HUSTLERS' LAW: RAISE THE RISK, RAISE THE PROFIT.

49. YOU DON'T NEED A YACHT—YOU JUST NEED A FRIEND WITH A YACHT!

50. I WAS TOLD I'D NEVER LIVE PAST TWENTY-ONE, SO EVERY DAY THAT I WAKE UP I'VE WON. I'M IN EXTRA INNINGS, BABY!

ABOUT THE AUTHORS

TRACY MARROW AKA ICE-T was born in New Jersey. As an only child whose parents died when he was very young, Ice-T became involved in Los Angeles gangs before spending four years in the army. He released a string of groundbreaking West Coast rap records and formed the thrash-metal band Body Count, whose 1991 self-titled debut contained the controversial single "Cop Killer." He currently stars as Detective Fin Tutuola on *Law & Order: SVU*.

DOUGLAS CENTURY is the author of *Barney Ross: The Life of a Jewish Fighter* and *Street Kingdom: Five Years Inside the Franklin Avenue Posse*, and is the co-author of the *New York Times* bestsellers *Takedown* and *Under and Alone*. He has written frequently for *The New York Times*, among many other publications, and is a contributing editor at *Tablet Magazine*.

ABOUT THE TYPE

This book was set in Garamond, a typeface designed by the French Printer Jean Jannon. It is styled after Garamond's original models. The face is dignified, and is light but without fragile lines. The italic is modeled after a font of Granjon, which was probably out in the middle of the sixteenth century.